First Printing: February 2015

I0142273

ISBN: 978-0692401293

Dedication

To my children: Ellie, Kyle, and Zach. I pray this will help you in pursuit of our Lord in your relationships.

Table of Contents

❧ ❧

Chapter 1: The True Purpose of Dating

> *""My son, give attention to my wisdom, incline your ear to my understanding; that you may observe discretion and your lips may reserve knowledge."*
> *Proverbs 5:1-2*

જીજી

We have all had the moment when our eyes connected with that guy or girl across the room; it was a magic moment. There was a rush of emotions when we saw him or her the first time. Butterflies swarmed in our stomachs when they walked by and we merely caught a glimpse of them. They were on our minds constantly and we dreamt of the next time we might see them. On the other end of the spectrum, most of us also know the heartache that comes when a relationship is ended badly. It is sad that many Christian organizations have enacted rules restricting members in the organization from dating each other because of the potential for drama that can occur, when the relationship is not pursued properly. It leaves us questioning whether it is even possible to date properly, without getting your heart broken. Is it really possible to break up with someone and not cause relational turmoil for us and others? I would answer with an emphatic "Yes," but only if the intentions for the relationship were spoken clearly from the outset and those intentions were continually reviewed to enable both people an opportunity to end the relationship amicably. Can we still date while still honoring God? Yes, but we must first know how to guard our hearts and the hearts of those we date against satanic attack and against our own physical desires, for that to be possible.

For over a decade now my wife and I have received and helped answer questions from many college students, who have been perplexed by these same questions. Most of them were individuals with a genuine desire to learn and obey Jesus' teaching; they just did not know where to find answers to these tough and important questions. They didn't think to look in the Bible, because they didn't know it said anything specific about dating, or they had never been told where to look for reliable answers. Most of them had never had a quality discussion with their parents about dating, and if they did, they didn't receive useful guidance. Answers they did receive were non-specific, such as, "Just have fun," or "Don't worry about that now, when it happens, it happens." Consequently, through trial and error, they have been stuck somewhere between the excited emotion of meeting someone new and the heartache of a bad breakup, unable to find an alternative.

Before God changed my ideas about dating, I treated my heart like a marshmallow on the end of a stick, plunging it into every relational campfire that would come along. In the end, I always ended up getting burned and I endured the heartache of a failed relationship. I often repeated the cycle of longing to be with someone, then experiencing infatuation and ultimately heartbreak. Strangely, I often began a new relationship to treat the heartache of the previous one. I constantly pushed the boundaries of what I knew was right in relationships, both physically and emotionally, leaving myself empty and disappointed. I eventually became dissatisfied with the thought of another dating relationship that might end badly; I was tired of getting my heart scorched, like the marshmallow too close to the fire. I refused to believe the lies Satan would tell me that I was useless, tainted or defective. I wanted a change. As a Christian learning how to live obedient to Jesus, I wanted to honor God in everything I did – but I didn't quite understand how to do that in the area of dating. I simply did not have a clear understanding of how to meet and relate to a girl in a dating situation.

I had many questions, but I didn't know where to find answers. I had been taught in church about the big "no-no's," such as

This book is not intended to be a formula for the perfect Christian relationship.

premarital sex, but what about everything else?? Could I kiss, hold hands, hug? What are the limits? What if I had already given myself physically to someone other than my spouse? What could I do to start living in obedience to Christ in my relationships today? How could I prepare for marriage today? Furthermore, how do I break up with someone anyway? Is there a better way than the "It's not you, it's me" cliché? I had Christian friends that I turned to for answers, but they had the same questions that I did. I may have picked up a few good ideas from a bible study or a sermon at church, but I never had anyone that I could work these ideas out with. I had no one to turn to except God and His Word. Through prayer and study, God slowly began to change my outlook on dating. Throughout this book, we will look at how we can apply Biblical principles for relationships to dating and how we can approach the dating relationships with confidence, by guarding our hearts and the hearts of those whom we date. This book is not intended to be a formula that explains how to act in every possible relationship. It does, however, discuss Biblically-based principles that should guide relationships… not just in the dating phase, but throughout life. At the end of the book, there is a list of the most commonly asked questions posed to my wife and me.

The Interview

Everybody has their reasons for dating. Some do it to have fun, to meet people, or even sadly, to get something from the other person, such as validation or sex. Some date because they are lonely, employing the first person who might

> *The true purpose of dating is to find your spouse.*

be a suitable short-term companion. Some remain in a dating relationship too long out of comfort, even though they are not interested in marrying the person they are dating. In the end, that kind of relationship becomes stagnant and unhealthy.

Let's take a step back to realize the true purpose of dating… finding the right person to marry. To date for any other reason is reckless and short-sighted, usually putting us in temptation's way, hindering our walk with Christ, and, ultimately, taking us further away from the goal of a fulfilling marriage to a great partner.

This is directed specifically to high school and college students, if you aren't ready or have no desire to get married in the next 6 to 12 months, don't date. Make friends, get to know people , be involved with people of both sexes in larger, group settings that don't lead to one-on-one entanglements and temptations of being alone with a person of the opposite sex… especially in your freshman year of college (see Chapter 6 for further discussion of this topic). If finding the best marriage partner isn't your goal in dating... what is?

We need to think of dating as an interview for marriage. This probably doesn't sound very romantic; it may not sound very spiritual. However it is the reason for dating. Consider an interview for a job. Interviews are instrumental in finding out more about the individual or person you are seeking to work with. This is when we (as the interviewer) learn about the person seeking the position and their qualifications. It is when we find out if they are suited for the position or if they need further training. It is also when we (as the interviewee) can see whether we fit into the organization, whether we can get along with those we will work with, and whether it was the position we had thought it was initially. Without the interview, both parties would be entering the relationship without enough useful information to make a good decision.

In every interview, there are a series of questions, usually prepared beforehand, that help guide the interview and help both parties to derive the most useful information from the interview. We will look at some questions to ask while dating, as well as some that you should ask yourself, in Chapter 2, "Seek Wisely". Those questions give us guidelines and help spark conversations to find out more about each other. The process became much clearer when God showed me that the purpose of dating was to find my wife, and in doing so, I was interviewing people to that end (and they were interviewing me). I was able to better evaluate the situation and whether the person I was dating was suited to be my mate (and I hers) rather than living in the emotion of the moment, feeling like I was "in love" which we will talk more about in the following chapters.

> *We need to think of dating as an interview for marriage.*

<u>*Take Home Points:*</u>

- *The true purpose of dating is to find your spouse.*

- *Our attitude toward dating should be that we are interviewing people for marriage.*

Chapter 2: Guarded Hearts

*"Watch over your heart with all diligence, for
from it flow the springs of life."*
Proverbs 4:23

৵৩

If you only view dating relationships as interviews for marriage that can still leave you open to heartache if you don't pursue them carefully. You must develop your way of thinking about, and your approach to the interview in such a way that will protect and shield your most valuable asset: your heart. After all, it is out of the heart that life springs forth.

Guarding Your Heart

Perhaps you are thinking... I've heard this before. The "guard your heart" phrase has been repeated so often in modern Christian culture that it has become a cliché. This is an ancient principle, however, and cannot be worn out with use. In the book of Proverbs, God tells us to guard our hearts. What does that look like practically and how can we apply it to dating relationships? When we hear the phrase "guard your heart" there is a tendency to only defend ourselves from the possibility of emotional pain or sin, instead of allowing God's divine protection to give us a greater sense of trust and relationship with our Lord. The command encourages us to:

> *Watch over your heart with all diligence, for from it flow the springs of life. Put away from you a deceitful mouth and put devious speech far from you. Let your eyes look directly ahead and let your gaze be fixed straight in front of you. Watch the path of your feet*

and all your ways will be established.
Do not turn to the right nor to the left;
turn your foot from evil.[1]

The word "heart" refers to the inner life of a person. In the heart dwell our feelings, emotions, desires and passions. It is the seat of all the forces and functions. The heart is where lust happens[2] and where our treasure is.[3] The heart is also the seat of understanding and the source of thought and reflection. It is where we form intent[4] and where we consider the complexity of life.[5] The heart is the seat of the will and the source of our resolves.[6] Therefore, our heart is an important part of our inner being; the

> *The word "heart" refers the center of the inner life of a man.*

---

[1] Proverbs 4:23-27
[2] Matthew 5:28
[3] Matthew 6:21
[4] Acts 8:22
[5] Luke 2:19
[6] John 13:2; Acts 11:23

center in which God moves, where our religious life is rooted, and where our moral conduct is chosen. That is why God is more interested in the internal workings of the heart, than in external performance, and not the outward appearance.[7]

> *We don't guard worthless things.*

An immortal soul has infinite value. This is the most central reason why it is necessary to guard our hearts, because our hearts are valuable. You are valuable! So valuable, that Christ willingly chose to give His life for you. Even if you have gone too far physically before marriage, even if you have given yourself sexually to someone other than your spouse, even if you have said things that you wish you could take back or done things to someone that should be reserved only for marriage… God still loves you. Remember, once you accept the sacrifice God made through the blood of Jesus and put your faith in Him, your sins are forgiven – all of them. God would not go to such extravagant lengths to get us back

---

[7] 1 Samuel 16:7

from the grips of hell, by sacrificing his own son to pay the debt of our sin, if we were worthless. For example, we don't care if someone steals our trash; that's why we take it out and sit it at the end of our driveways, unguarded. We don't guard worthless things. Knowing that your Creator valued you enough to die for you brings a new sense of self-worth, and knowing that it was not of your own doing diminishes

> *God doesn't see you as ruined!*

arrogance. The heart is the center of who you are, and how you connect with other people and God. If your heart has been wounded because of improper relationships, it can harm your relationship with your future spouse and other Christians. For this reason, God says to guard your heart above all else. If you have engaged in improper relationships, whether physical or emotional, prior to marriage, please don't stop reading – God does not see you as ruined, and neither will your spouse! New opportunities are given to us each new day. We will discuss how you can have

God-honoring relationships and how you can start living a life that glorifies God.

God says that from the heart "flow the springs of life," meaning that the heart is the source of everything else in our lives. Jesus says that what we speak comes from our hearts.[8] Our heart overflows into our thoughts and our actions. Just as poisoning a water well will affect many people, if we don't guard our spring of life from spiritually and physically toxic things, it will negatively affect our lives. A damaged heart threatens our relationships with our friends, our

> *Satan is out to destroy the life that wells up within our hearts.*

ministry to others, our future family and our relationship with God. There is a long list of things, from lust to greed, that Satan brings into our path to corrupt our hearts. Satan doesn't just oppose God, but also everything that is aligned with God... that includes us. Jesus says, "The thief comes only to steal

---

[8] Matthew 15:18

and kill and destroy; I came that they may have life, and have it abundantly."[9] Since that verse is true, it indicates that Satan is out to destroy our lives. When we have an enemy that is precisely focused on our destruction, we would do well by guarding our hearts against him. Satan attacks our hearts in countless ways, such as disappointment, discouragement, false expectations, and most often, those feelings will be prompted by those who are closest to us. In dating, the attack comes physically, through sexual temptation or abuse, and emotionally, when we give our hearts to one it wasn't meant for; this all causes heartbreak when the relationship is over.

We shouldn't be motivated to guard our hearts out of fear of sin because that ultimately leads us to a lack of empathy and love for those around us. Our desire to guard our hearts should come from the life that God has given us and the desire to keep the source of that life healthy. Remember, especially when speaking about dating, we are guarding our hearts - not hoarding emotions. God doesn't say to turn our foot

---

[9] John 10:10

from *people*, he says to guard our hearts by turning our foot from *evil*.[10] We aren't supposed to take ourselves out of the world; quite the opposite, we are supposed to go into the world and show those around us who our Lord is, by living the way Jesus would. We should, however, limit the access others have to our hearts by guarding our hearts. That doesn't mean we withhold affection. It means we withhold inappropriate access to our hearts. Inappropriate access to our hearts is when we let someone into our hearts, either emotionally, by giving our hearts to them, or physically, by engaging in premarital sex. This is access that was meant only for our spouses. This is why, if we desire to date successfully, without the drama and heartache, and flourish later in marriage, we must guard our hearts by having the correct priorities and a right view of dating.

Praying for Your Spouse

When I was in college at Texas A&M

---

[10] Proverbs 4:27

University, I had many odd jobs to make ends meet. The summer before my senior year I began a job with a neurology professor in the College of Veterinary Sciences, creating a computer program for his neuroanatomy course. It was a great job for a student, because it allowed me to work when I wanted and how I wanted. A few years after giving my life to Christ, I began to examine issues that faced me in a new way. I knew that I needed to seek strong Christian role models whom I could emulate, and this job provided me with the opportunity to listen to archived radio shows of *Focus on the Family* with Dr. James Dobson, while I worked. I am not sure how many of those broadcasts I heard, but I can tell you that I listened to every one they had available, and I tried to internalize every bit of wisdom. In one of the broadcasts, I remember vividly Dr. Dobson describing how his great-grandfather, G. W. McCluskey, spent the hour between 11:00 a.m. and noon every day in prayer, and how he fasted on Thursdays and prayed for the spiritual welfare of his family – his children, grandchildren and great-grandchildren – before they were even born. Dr. Dobson had this to say about his family's spiritual heritage:

> *"The McCluskeys had two girls, one of whom was my grandmother and the other, my great-aunt. Both grew up and married ministers in the denomination of their father and mother. Between these women, five girls and one boy were born. One of them was my mother. All five of the girls married ministers in the denomination of their grandfather, and the boy became one. That brought it down to my generation. My cousin H. B. London and I were the first to go through college, and we were roommates. In the beginning of our sophomore year, he announced that God was calling him to preach. And I can assure you, I began to get very nervous about the family tradition! I never felt God was asking me to be a*

minister, so I went to graduate school and became a psychologist. And yet, I have spent my professional life speaking, teaching, and writing about the importance of my faith in Jesus Christ. At times as I sit on a platform waiting to address a church filled with Christians, I wonder if my great-grandfather isn't smiling at me from somewhere. His prayers have reached across four generations of time to influence what I am doing with my life day by day."[11]

What an incredible legacy he left behind! As I heard this message I felt moved to do the same, but I added my wife into the prayer… after all, she would be an integral part in starting a family. I began to pray that my wife would have a strong walk with Christ, and

---

[11] Dr. James Dobson http://drjamesdobson.org/Solid-Answers/Answers?a=e4174a3f-c2f0-4a6b-8e47-97bb8c915458#sthash.mpjix6bd.dpuf

that she would remain faithful to me and to her Lord. I prayed for her to have integrity and the ability to lead and be led. I prayed that my children would come to know the Lord early in life, and that they would live to glorify the name of Jesus. I also prayed that our household would be conducive to the development of my children's faith, and that we would be able to pass on our faith to them. I prayed for their children, my grandchildren that the Lord would use me in such a way in their lives, and the lives of others, that it would impact them for generations to come. I prayed that my grandchildren, would not only keep their faith in the Lord, but advance that faith.

As I began to pray and fast, as Mr. McCluskey had done so many years before, my heart began to change. The way I viewed dating up to that time was no different than my non-Christian friends - that is, mostly to "have

> *As I read the Bible, I learned what qualities God thought I should look for in my wife.*

fun." Through those times of prayer, God changed my heart and gave me insight into dating and finding my wife. From that point on, I intentionally guarded my heart from anything that could damage my relationship with the Lord and my future wife. As I read the Bible, I learned what qualities God thought I should look for in my wife, and what I needed to change to prepare myself to be a husband and, ultimately, a father. During those times of prayer I learned principles for dating that I discuss in this book. I want to encourage you to start today to pray for your spouse and your children, whether you are a teenager just starting to discover the complexities of life or a single thirty-something. It will change who you are and how you view the opposite sex. It will have a far reaching spiritual effects on you and your family for generations to come.

Priorities Dictate Our Lives

Recently, on a crisp, Fall Saturday morning, I was late getting out of the house to attend a Christian

> *Whatever we are willing to put off for something else is the lower priority.*

conference. I felt rushed and tired… no matter how much sleep I had the night before. On the way there I thought, "I'm dead. I could use a Starbucks right about now… I think they have that Pumpkin Spice Latte… I need one of those!" So, one "venti" latte and oversized muffin later, I walk into the conference obnoxiously late, sporting a coffee mustache and crumbs on my shirt. Luckily, I was only attending and was not the speaker!

My priority that morning was not to get to the conference on time but to get coffee and breakfast. That is exactly how priorities in our lives can be assessed. Whatever we are willing to put off for something else is the lower priority. That is how we can quickly assess what the true priorities are in our lives. I was willing to put off getting to the conference on time for a caffeine/sugar fix. The coffee was a higher priority. Our priorities ultimately dictate our choices. They control how much time we spend on projects, when we go places, who we go with, what we spend our money on, and many more behaviors. When our priorities are correct, we filter our lives by them, keeping the important areas of our life as the primary factors in making decision and the less important areas from taking control.

There is an extensive list of things competing for our attention: work, school, friends, love interests, family, the organizations we belong to, hobbies, sports, even our church activities. Because the ultimate authorities in our lives should be God's Word and His Holy Spirit, our challenge is to develop a biblical framework from which to prioritize our lives. The first of the Ten Commandments tells us that we shall have no other gods ahead of God Himself.[12] It States:

> *"You shall not make for yourself an idol, or any likeness of what is in heaven above or on the earth beneath or in the water under the earth. You*

---

[12] Exodus 20:3

> *shall not worship them or serve them;*
> *for I, the LORD your God, am a jealous*
> *God"[13]*

It is obvious that, according to God's Word, we must always keep God as our first priority. Yet how many things in that long list that occupy our time, thoughts, money and attention have taken the place of God in our lives?

Before you can have a proper dating relationship with *any* human being, you need to have the proper relationship with God through His Son Jesus Christ. That includes allowing Him to be first in our lives at all times. Jesus says, "Seek first His kingdom and His righteousness, and all these things will be added to you."[14] You

> *You should make it your goal to have a deep, intimate relationship with God.*

---

[13] Deuteronomy 5:8-9
[14] Matthew 6:33

should make it your goal to have a deep, intimate relationship with God—one where you don't just ask for things in prayer, as if he were a genie, but listen to what he wants from you. Your desire for a closer relationship with God should lead you to study His Word, to discern what He wants you to believe, allowing Him into every area of your life… including dating. If you tend to primarily look to other people for answers and validation, pray and ask the Lord to help you look to Him instead.

The apostle Paul addressed what our true motivation should be when he wrote, "but just as we have been approved by God to be entrusted with the gospel, so we speak, not as pleasing men, but God who examines our hearts." [15] He also wrote, "Whether, then, you eat or drink or whatever you do, do all to the glory of God." [16] When we are motivated to glorify God's name above our own, and live to please God instead of man, He promises to bless our lives and make us prosper. The psalmist says of the righteous

---

[15] 1 Thessalonians 2:4
[16] 1 Corinthians 10:31

man, "He will be like a tree firmly planted by streams of water, which yields its fruit in its season and its leaf does not wither; and in whatever he does, he prospers."[17] A biblical worldview requires us to place God's commands and values as the controlling principles in our lives. In order to assess whether we have placed something else above God, it can help to ask ourselves this question every day, "What am I not willing to give up, if God asked?" Like my earlier example, I wasn't willing to give up coffee and breakfast to be on time; therefore it had a higher priority in my life. Whatever it is that you aren't willing to give up is above God in your list of priorities. We have to be willing to trust God with everything, in the same way that Abraham was willing to trust God with the life of his own son.[18]

Although our society has done much to undermine the importance of the family, it should be our next highest priority after our relationship to God. There is nothing on earth that is more important than

---

[17] Psalm 1:3
[18] Genesis 22:1-18

family. Paul tells us that men are to love their wives as Christ loved the church... to the point of death to protect her.[19] Christ's first priority was obeying the Father in order to glorify Him. His bride, the church, is his second priority.[20] Jesus lived his entire earthly life and sacrificed himself in preparation for the future union with the church, his bride. In the same way, wives are to put themselves under the authority of their husbands "as to the Lord."[21] This is not a rule, but a principle that says a woman's responsibilities in her relationship to her husband are second only to her responsibilities to God in her priorities. If you are to follow the example of Christ, your spouse should be second only to God... even if you are not married. So, God is your first priority, and your family (spouses being the founding member of your immediate family) is second only to Him. Since a husband and wife are one flesh[22] the logical conclusion is that your children, the result of the marriage bond, should be your next

---

[19] Ephesians 5:25
[20] Revelation 19:7-9; 21:1-2
[21] Ephesians 5:22
[22] Ephesians 5:31

priority. That, again, applies, even if you aren't dating anyone or don't have children.

God tells us to honor our parents so that we would live fuller lives... it is noteworthy that there is no age restriction specified here.[23] The lack of an age limit shows us that we should honor our parents as long as they are living on earth with us. Thus we come to our next priority under family, our parents. Paul tells us that, "if anyone does not provide for his own, and especially for those of his household, he has denied the faith and is worse than an unbeliever."[24] So after God, our family is our second priority. First our spouse, then our children, parents, and extended families. When we keep those priorities, even now when we aren't married, God begins to

> *If you are to follow the example of Christ, your spouse should be second only to God... even if you aren't married.*

---

[23] Deuteronomy 5:16
[24] 1 Timothy 5:8

change us for the better. It changes how we view dating – we begin to guard our heart for our future spouse.

After God and our family, our next priority should be our brothers and sisters in Christ. Paul tells us not to put a stumbling block or hindrance in the way of our brother[25], and instructs us to serve one another in love.[26] He also instructs us to encourage one another and build each other up.[27] After our families, we should be concerned with our spiritual families, our churches, and then, finally, everyone else. Jesus commands us to go and make disciples of all the nations.[28] So, for clarity, here is what our priority list should look like according to what the Bible teaches:

---

[25] Ephesians 14:13
[26] Galatians 5:13
[27] 1 Thessalonians 5:11
[28] Matthew 28:19

1. God
2. Family
   a. Spouse (husband or wife)
   b. Children
   c. Parents
   d. Extended Family
3. Church Family
4. Everyone Else

When you have to make critical decisions in life, you make them based on your priorities, right or wrong. When you have to decide where to focus our time and energy, a Biblical model of priorities keeps you from neglecting the relationships that are most important. If you keep your husband or wife as second in your life under God, even if you aren't married, and your children third, it will be much harder for you to become sexually involved with the person you are dating because your focus is on your spouse and your kids, automatically guarding your heart. Furthermore, by keeping your priorities in line, starting today, you will be much better off in the beginning years of marriage because you have already developed a life pattern to do so. There will be much less likelihood of your parents coming in between you and your spouse because you have been guarding your heart and preparing it for that moment years prior. Likewise, when your children try to manipulate you and your spouse, your heart is ready for it, and you won't put your kids above your spouse.

Fortify the Protection

We have discussed the power of praying for your spouse, the purpose of dating and why it is important to approach it with the correct motives, and how our priorities shape who we are and how we decide. These fundamental concepts can help change our thinking about dating. When I started to work out these principles in my life, I became aware of how poorly I had guarded my own heart in the past. I began to realize that the reason I had such a hard time getting over breakups was because I had given access to areas of my heart that were meant only for my wife by giving them the position, or priority, in my heart that was meant only for my wife. Consequently, when they were no longer there taking that place, my heart would ache – and while this is understood to be a figurative term, it would literally manifest itself in my life through symptoms of stress – like tension headaches and heartburn. We have likely all been there. As I prayed through this, I asked the Lord to show me how to fortify the protection of my heart; to help make the guarding of my heart stronger and more immediate. As I was praying through this, one idea that came into my mind was to write letters to my future wife. As a college guy, writing letters to my future wife seemed like a pretty girly act, and wasn't an easy thing to hear, much less do. Just the thought of it was uncomfortable and awkward. I thought, "How on earth am I going to write to someone I don't even know?" I didn't keep the letters I wrote at first; I just wrote them and either threw them away or deleted them from my computer after typing them. Eventually, I realized that, by writing these letters, I was practicing the principles I was learning from the Bible about how I should view the opposite sex - not as an object but as a person, someone's wife.

On November 18, 1999, the rubber met the road. I was excited that whole week, because that Thursday morning, on the 18th, I was going to pick up my Aggie ring (that's the class ring all students receive when they finish their junior year). Other than graduation, Aggie Ring Day is the biggest day in the life of a student at Texas A&M. That morning, however, was darkened by a tragedy.

Every fall, an enormous bonfire was built to be burned on the evening before the football game with the University of Texas. At the time, it was almost 60 feet tall, consisting of about 5000 huge logs. That morning, it collapsed during construction. Of the 58 students and former students working on the stack, 12 were killed and 27 were injured, some of them were friends of mine. That day after receiving my class ring, I stood at the site where the stack had fallen, witnessing the heartbreak of parents and friends involved. When I went home that evening, I was emotionally numb and sat down to write out my

> *I began by addressing the letters to "My Wife"…*

thoughts. I hadn't planned to write to my future wife, but that's what happened. I began by addressing the letter to "My Wife" and I shared with her the events of the day, how it had made me feel and what the impact was. I shared with her the commitment I had made to our family, to pray for our children and for her. It was at that time I decided to save the letters for my wife and give them to her on our honeymoon. For better or worse, she would now be able to share in the experiences I had before knowing her, as well as know the lengths I took to protect my heart for her.

I continued writing these letters to her; most of them short, encapsulated thoughts such as, "Went to [fill in the blank], wish you were here to experience it with me," or, "Met a girl today, wondered if it was you," even, "Stopped seeing a girl today because she wasn't you – now we're one step closer." Sometimes, but not often, I would write lengthy letters, detailing lessons God had been teaching me or what He was calling me to do.

Then came the day when I actually found out who my wife was. It was a pretty amazing feeling to finally be able to address the letter to the woman I knew I would marry. The letter, published with her permission, follows:

To Amanda,

I never thought this day would come. Last night, Sunday, January 2, 2000 at 1:00 a.m. I found myself wide awake, praying and God impressed upon my heart that you were the one. I am so happy!

I Will Love You Forever,
Ryan

When we arrived home from our honeymoon, we exchanged gifts. I have a picture of Amanda the moment after she read that letter, with tears in her eyes. Writing those letters to her began as an exercise in shaping my heart; teaching me how to rightly view dating, women, and helping me to put my priorities in order. In the end, it became a powerful witness to my wife, showing her the lengths I was willing to go to protect her and our family. Even today, when there is an issue that seems insurmountable in our marriage (which happens in every marriage), I can point to that box of letters and remind her that I have always been committed to her, and I will always be committed to her. The groundwork for a successful marriage was laid when I wrote her that first letter.

The Effect of Guarding Your Heart

King Solomon was the wisest man who ever lived.[29] In the book of Proverbs, he shares that wisdom and instruction with his sons, writing:

Watch over your heart with all

---

[29] 1 Kings 3:12

diligence, for from it flow the springs of life.[30]

Notice that there is no age constraint here! We need to be disciplined at guarding our hearts our entire lives – the earlier we start practicing this, the better. If we

> *If we become skilled early in life before marriage, it becomes much easier to ward off adultery when we are married.*

become skilled early in life before marriage, it becomes much easier to resist adultery when we are married. Jesus instructs us, "Be on guard, so that your hearts will not be weighted down with dissipation and drunkenness and the worries of life, and that day will not come on you suddenly like a trap; for it will come upon all those who dwell on the face of all the earth."[31] So, by taking an active role in guarding our hearts, we

---

[30] Proverbs 4:23
[31] Luke 21:34-35

put ourselves in a better place to listen to God during the times when life becomes difficult; once again – fortifying the protection of our hearts.

The best way I have found to assess where I am in this process is to ask God. At the end of every day, I ask Him, "Did I live today to glorify your name or mine? Did I protect my heart today?" and, "How can I protect it more completely?" If we ask and take time to listen, He will tell us. If you haven't yet asked Jesus into your heart, accepting the sacrifice He made by dying to pay the debt of your sin, today is as good a time as any. Start guarding your heart today for God and for your future spouse tomorrow.

Take Home Points:

- *You must guard your heart, limiting access that was meant for our spouses.*

- *Praying for your future spouse can change how you view those you date and help protect you.*

- *Your priorities dictate how you live.*

- *God should be your first priority.*

- *Your future spouse should be your second priority, even if you are not yet married.*

- *You can help focus your priorities and fortify the protection of your heart by writing letters to your future spouse.*

Chapter 3: Seek Wisely

*Do not be bound together with unbelievers; for
what partnership have righteousness and
lawlessness, or what fellowship has light with
darkness?*
2 Corinthians 6:14

❧❧

Viewing the dating relationship as an interview
for marriage is just the beginning. After creating and
fortifying the protection of our hearts, we need to set
up parameters for that interview: the applicant
qualifications, job description, and a way to evaluate
the applicants based on those parameters. Let's use the
principles set out in God's Word to seek our spouse
wisely.

Get to Know Them From Afar

College students often tell me that they think the Bible is silent on dating. My usual reply to that assessment is that the Bible says as much about dating as it does about the Trinity... just because the word "Trinity" isn't used in the Bible, doesn't mean that it isn't an important doctrine. Likewise, because the word "dating" isn't used in the Bible, doesn't mean that there aren't sound principles to follow in dating relationships. Dating, while a fairly modern activity, is a prelude to marriage, so we should look at what God says wives and husbands should act like in order to gain insight to the qualities of the person we should aspire to marry. More importantly, we should use those qualities to show us what kind of character we need to develop to be the men and women God wants us to be.

It is best to try to find out as much about the person as possible at a distance... and I'm not talking about "Facebook

> *The less you get romantically involved with someone who isn't your spouse, the better off you will be in marriage.*

stalking." Chances are you know people around the person you are interested in. Before pursuing a dating relationship with them, try to gather as much information, and answer as many of the questions we will pose in the following sections as possible; it could very well save you some heartache. Remember, the less you get romantically involved with someone who isn't your future spouse, the better off you will be.

What do we need to look for? Many people have chosen to construct a "check-list" of qualities they would like their future spouse to have, although many of them include external things like eye color and hair color. What do you think God's checklist looks like for your spouse? What do you think God,

> *Dating is an interview for marriage.*

who created you by forming you in your mother's womb [32] and values you greatly, would put on His "check-list" of requirements that he wants the spouse of his son or daughter to have? It just so happens that God gave us just such a list.

Meet the Job Requirements

At the bare minimum, the first thing we should look at in a prospective spouse is their relationship with Christ. Remember that dating is primarily an interview for marriage. You want the man or woman that will be with you for the rest of your life to share your same religious beliefs and habits. You should be sure his or her core convictions produce godly behavior and character. Paul says, "Do not be bound together with unbelievers; for what partnership have

---

[32] Psalm 139:13

righteousness and lawlessness, or what fellowship has light with darkness?"[33] That's easy to understand. Never be bound in any relationship with an unbeliever. This does not mean you can't have friends who are unbelievers. One could argue that the twelve disciples were not believers in Jesus at the time He called them to follow Him. Paul is saying that binding yourself, whether in a business partnership, dating relationship or especially marriage, to an unbeliever will ultimately end in discord. This discord is caused by the two partners having different core beliefs, resulting in a lack of unity. Secondly, you should never expect any person, a non-believer or a Christian, to change just because you are dating them. Many marriages have ended in divorce because of expectations that a man or woman would magically transform into what the other wanted. Therefore, the first important factor is that the person you date should know Jesus

Never be bound in any relationship with an unbeliever.

---

[33] 2 Corinthians 6:14

as his or her Lord and Savior and demonstrate evidence of their belief in the way they speak and act.

In every dating relationship there is that initial attraction. The day I met Amanda, who would later become my wife, I was at a fraternity rush event outside one of the dormitory cafeterias on campus. I remember being struck by how pretty she was. She came by because she was supposed to eat lunch with one of the fraternity brothers I was with, but it turned out that he had already eaten. She turned and asked if anyone else wanted to grab lunch, and I, in a sheepishly brave voice, raised my hand and said, "I will!" There are qualities that you naturally gravitate toward and find beautiful in the opposite sex. That is how God made us to respond to each other. However, to make a decision on who to date based solely on what they look like does not prepare us well for the dating process. Solomon puts it like this, "Charm is deceitful and beauty is vain, but a woman who fears the LORD, she shall be praised."[34]

Everyone gets old, and everyone's body

---

[34] Proverbs 31:30

changes. After a few years of marriage, you don't want to be married to this beautiful person if you share no interests, can't carry on enjoyable conversations, and don't enjoy her companionship. What endures, even grows over time, is our long-term attraction to a person's personality, character and attitude. That is when we know all the good and bad about the person and still want to be with them for life. If you want someone to love you for who you are, and not just what you look like, then don't focus solely on outward appearance. The first, most important, and completely non-negotiable quality you should look for in your mate is whether he or she has an active, vibrant walk with the Lord. Are they obeying the teachings of Jesus in the daily, practical decisions of life?

What the Bible Says to Look for in a Man

Ok ladies, let's get specific on what you should look for in a man. First off, the guy that you are looking for has to be capable of, and willing to, lead you spiritually. What that looks like in a dating relationship is that, at any point, you should be able to say that you are in a better relationship with Christ because of knowing him. In other words, will this guy bring you closer to or take you further from your Lord? The man has a responsibility not to hinder, but also to enable your relationship with Jesus. Specifically, you should look at what qualities God says leaders should have.

There are quite a few instructions in the Bible that explain how men should carry themselves, and they are great for ladies to study in order to know what they should look for, and for men to study to find out what they need to emulate. Some of them aren't gender specific and can apply to both men and women, so we will look at both. Paul writes to Titus and tells him how both older and younger men should act,

> *The man has a responsibility not to hinder, but to enable your relationship with Jesus.*

saying:

> *Older men are to be temperate,*
> *dignified, sensible, sound in faith, in*
> *love, in perseverance... Likewise urge*
> *the young men to be sensible; in all*
> *things show yourself to be an example*
> *of good deeds, with purity in doctrine,*
> *dignified, sound in speech which is*
> *beyond reproach, so that the opponent*
> *will be put to shame, having nothing*
> *bad to say about us.*[35]

That's a good list! That section of scripture defines what a godly Christian should look like. If the guy you want to date is dignified, showing self-restraint, is biblically sound (that is, he doesn't just go to church once in a while, but actively reads and applies God's Word), does good and no one can say anything bad about him, these are good indicators that this one is the right sort of person to be interested in.

---

[35] Titus 2:3, 6-8

Paul speaks to the church at Ephesus, saying:

> *But immorality or any impurity or greed must not even be named among you, as is proper among saints; and there must be no filthiness and silly talk, or coarse jesting, which are not fitting, but rather giving of thanks.*[36]

The word translated "immorality" is the Greek word "porneia," from which we derive the word "pornography" ... need I explain further? Not only should the guy you are dating be sexually pure, he shouldn't even be joking about this area. Kidding around about sexually explicit topics is a guaranteed symptom of deeper, darker things going on inside a man's heart. Christians aren't immune to the temptation to view pornography. A survey reported by *Leadership Journal* written by Christianity Today, revealed that half of Christian pastors (51%) say Internet pornography is a possible temptation for

---

[36] Ephesians 5:3-4

them, while 37 percent admit it is a current struggle (the remaining 12% are either lying or in foolish denial of its potential power over them).[37] Be wary of men who show the heart symptom of constant, perverse joking; it can only mean that they have deeper issues. Secondly, James calls the tongue a fire that can be used for good or evil.[38] You want to have a relationship with a man in which he will use the force of his words for good in your life and in the lives of others. If he speaks well of you and those around you, he will likely also do so in marriage.

How a man views his job is a great way to see how he will handle his role in supporting a family. Paul, writing to a young

> *Be wary of men who show the heart symptom of constant, perverse joking; it can only mean that they have deeper issues.*

---

[37] "The Leadership Survey on Pastors and Internet Pornography." Leadership Journal: Real Ministry In A Complex World Winter 2001: n. page. Print.

[38] James 3:6

pastor named Timothy, says, "Be diligent to present yourself approved to God as a workman who does not need to be ashamed, accurately handling the word of truth."[39] Paul is speaking about how he should be diligent in his work ethic; not only so that he would study the Word of God and relate it accurately to his church members, but that they would see that quality in him and be challenged to do the same. On the other hand, there has always been this Hollywood idea that women love the "bad boys" who, ironically, are the exact type of men who can't support and cherish a woman for the rest of her life. Paul tells Titus, "Remind them to be subject to rulers, to authorities, to be obedient, to be ready for every good deed."[40] To put it bluntly, if he doesn't follow the law, you don't want to follow him. Don't even be associated with him because you won't change him, and he doesn't want to be changed.

Paul gives us the virtues of a leader in the church. He says:

---

[39] 2 Timothy 2:15
[40] Titus 3:1

For the overseer must be above reproach as God's steward, not self-willed, not quick-tempered, not addicted to wine, not pugnacious, not fond of sordid gain, but hospitable, loving what is good, sensible, just, devout, self-controlled, holding fast the faithful word which is in accordance with the teaching, so that he will be able both to exhort in sound doctrine and to refute those who contradict.[41]

Look for a man who is not just above reproach, but above reproach as God's steward. That means that he is not only a Christian, but he is obeying the New Testament commands on how to live like Jesus, and it is visible to those around him. He should be selfless and even-tempered. He shouldn't have an addiction and he should love what is right, being devout in his faith and able and willing to articulate it to others. In

---

[41] Titus 1:7-9

short, he should walk in the same manner Jesus walked.[42]

Most women like a sense of humor, and we have already talked about "course jesting," but how does that fit into God's list? Paul says, "When I was a child, I used to speak like a child, think like a child, reason like a child; when I became a man, I did away with childish things."[43] Please do not misunderstand – if you value a sense of humor, be sure to marry a man who has the capacity to be child-like, not childish! Just because we grow up and become adults, doesn't mean that we can't have fun anymore. My wife and I have a blast on date nights doing the most random things, like riding on shopping carts in parking lots or singing a song as loud as possible (usually not that well). We enjoy having fun

> *It isn't alright to revert to a childish state of self-centeredness and selfishness.*

---

[42] 1 John 2:6
[43] 1 Corinthians 13:11

like kids; child-like fun. It is okay to let loose and have a good time. What isn't alright, and what Paul is referring to, is when a man (or woman) reverts to a childish state of self-centeredness and selfishness. As a man, it is not okay to shirk responsibility and abdicate responsibility to others. It is not okay to refuse to grow as a Christian. If you marry a man who is childish, as opposed to child-like, you will be forever having to do for him what he should be doing for you, because what he really wants is a mommy or a receptive audience, not a wife. If you marry a man who is not beyond this adolescent mindset he will be too self-centered to ever cherish you the way you need to be cherished.

To sum up these qualities, you should look for a man who has his priorities in order, keeps God first in his life, enjoys his relationship with the Lord and obeys New Testament teaching about living out our faith accurately. He needs to be sensible and morally sound. A man with those qualities would look a lot like this.

> *Therefore be imitators of God, as beloved children; and walk in love, just as Christ also loved you and gave Himself up for us, an offering and a sacrifice to God as a fragrant aroma.*[44]

> *If he isn't willing to sacrifice to follow God today, you shouldn't expect him to do so in marriage.*

If he is trying to imitate God and values others above himself, he will do the same for you. If he isn't willing to follow God today, you shouldn't expect him to do so in marriage. When you are praying for your future husband, pray with these qualities in mind. Pray that your future husband would keep his priorities, be consistently obedient to the commands from scripture, be willing to keep his family ahead of his occupation, that he would live a life completely surrendered to God's authority, and daily glorify God.

---

[44] Ephesians 5:1

You should have a physical attraction to someone, but notice that nowhere in these verses did God say, "Look for the guy with washboard abs." While physical attraction is usually the first thing that draws you to someone, it should not be the sole basis for dating someone. Neither should the income level or the social status of his family be the primary basis for determining who you date. While all three should be taken into consideration, God's list should come first. Obviously, if your dad was the C.E.O. of a Fortune 500 company with a high income and was able to provide the many material comforts for you that will develop expectations about what your husband should eventually be able to provide for you. There is no rule that says you can't marry a janitor with a small salary, but know that it could cause issues in your marriage, and seek guidance from your pastor or a Christian counselor who can help you both think through the obstacles before you enter into marriage.

So, here is a list traits that God says helps to make godly husbands:

- Consistently obedient Christian (doesn't just go to church but actively pursues Christ)
- Self-controlled
- Respected
- Morally pure
- Hard worker, yet doesn't put his job ahead of God or his family
- Obedient heart (to God and the law)
- Not childish or selfish
- Protects his heart
- Physically attractive to you

Before you pursue a serious relationship with someone, make sure he meets these criterion to your satisfaction. If not, break off the dating relationship quickly and respectfully and avoid inevitable heartache later.

What the Bible Says to Look for in a

Woman

It shouldn't be groundbreaking when I say that men are visually stimulated. God created men to be stimulated at the sight of a woman. Women are relational; men are experiential. For the most part, women fantasize about the marriage (putting the guy's last name with their first name to see what it sounds like, what the wedding will be like, etc.). Guys fantasize about sex. Does that mean that guys don't

> *Women fantasize about the wedding, guys fantasize about sex.*

get emotionally involved, or that women aren't attracted physically to guys? Of course not, but as a general rule, guys are more visually stimulated than girls. God makes women attractive to men, like flowers to bees, however once you are attracted to the beauty of a particular woman, you need to quickly evaluate other areas of character and behavior. While physical attraction is important, it should never be the sole determining factor in whether to start a relationship with a girl. Let me say this again for clarity, you need to be physically attracted to the girl you are pursuing, understanding the way men are constructed, but then you must think through the rest of the Bible's list for godly women that we are about to discuss. Remember the proverb that says, "Charm is deceitful and beauty is vain, but a woman who fears the Lord, she shall be praised."[45]

When I first met my wife, I was, and still am to this day, captivated by her beauty. She is literally the most beautiful woman I have ever met. However, it wasn't only her physical beauty that captivated me, and it certainly wasn't the sole basis of our relationship, nor is it why I wanted to marry her. If her physical beauty was the only thing that attracted me to her, as we grew older and our bodies changed, I would have lost the attraction for her altogether. There must be more to the attraction` than physical. You should be attracted to who she is, in addition to what she looks

---

[45] Proverbs 31:30

like, otherwise you will find yourself in a relationship with someone in whom you have nothing in common. Peter addresses the women in the church saying:

> *Your adornment must not be merely external—braiding the hair, and wearing gold jewelry, or putting on dresses; but let it be the hidden person of the heart, with the imperishable quality of a gentle and quiet spirit, which is precious in the sight of God.*[46]

Gentlemen, herein lies our first set of criterion. The girl you want to date (and eventually marry) can't be, to put it in racing terms, "all chrome and no engine." My room-mates in college used to call these "girls

> *Be attracted to her heart, her "gentle spirit," not the façade of what she wears or how she makes herself up.*

---

[46] 1 Peter 3:3-4

with a gimmick." These were girls that weren't really all that fun to hang around, didn't have much personality or a walk with God, but they dressed themselves up and made themselves attractive (hence the gimmick) in order to make themselves more appealing. Guys, that isn't the girl you want, and ladies, that isn't the girl you want to be. Guys, you want to find the girl who is just as comfortable in a T-shirt and jeans as she is in a formal gown. In addition to your attraction to her physical beauty, you need to be attracted to her as a person, her "gentle spirit."

Paul was a mentor to many men in the first century church. We have letters he wrote to two of those mentees: Timothy and Titus. Writing to Timothy, he says, "Women must likewise be dignified, not malicious gossips, but temperate, faithful in all things."[47] The girl you want to date should be worthy of respect, should not have a heart for slandering others, should be restrained and not brash, and should be faithful to God and to her parents.

Paul goes on further in his letter to Titus to say:

---

[47] 1 Timothy 3:11

> *Older women likewise are to be*
> *reverent in their behavior, not*
> *malicious gossips nor enslaved to*
> *much wine, teaching what is good, so*
> *that they may encourage the young*
> *women to love their husbands, to love*
> *their children, to be sensible, pure,*
> *workers at home, kind, being subject to*
> *their own husbands, so that the word of*
> *God will not be dishonored.*[48]

Again, Paul says women shouldn't be brash, meaning rude, pushy and arrogant. A brash woman, or man for that matter, has a tendency to put others off. Don't confuse being brash with being confident. Women, who are confident in themselves, without being arrogant, are incredibly attractive to men; men are attracted to confidence. Women shouldn't be addicted to alcohol; if they are, you can bet it will be an issue in marriage. Most couples who marry eventually have children, so the girl you want to look for should have

---

[48] Titus 2:3-5

> *When Christian homes don't function as God intends, it is a horrible witness to those outside the church.*

a caring attitude toward children. She should be sensible and prudent, with money and in speech. She should be kind and able to be led. Some translations have "submit" instead of "being subject" which has caused much tension over the years from men misapplying the scripture. The Greek word used there is "hypotasso" which means "to put one's self under another's authority." The picture in the Greek is when one field general in battle puts himself under the direction of another field general to accomplish a common goal. Both have equal rank and say in decisions, but one makes a conscious decision to place himself under the other's authority to accomplish a greater task. Ladies, the message there is that you have to be willing to place yourself under the spiritual leadership of your husband (notice I didn't say boyfriend – the Bible *never* says to submit to anyone but your husband or your parents) and gentlemen, you have to strive to be someone worth following. If the man is not leading spiritually by following his Lord, the woman won't want to follow him. That causes discord in the marriage relationship, and according to Paul, causes the Word of God to be dishonored. Indeed, when Christian homes don't function as God intends, it is a horrible witness to those outside the church.

One of the clearest passages in the Bible about wives is Proverbs 31:10-31. This industrious woman is prized because she is trustworthy and does only good to her husband. Trustworthiness is key in any relationship, but to a man, trust is paramount. She is described as being a hard worker and a good steward. Disagreement over money is one of the most common issues identified as a reason for divorce, so you need to be sure she is a good steward of her money (or her parent's money) today, or she won't be a good steward of money in marriage tomorrow. The woman is described as responsible, wise, caring, and taking good care of her family. Most married couples eventually have children. If you want to have a family, one thing you should observe and evaluate is whether or not the person you are dating would be a good mother. You do that by seeing how she treats younger kids (siblings, cousins, etc.). You could babysit with them or volunteer in your church's children's Sunday school.

These verses give us a great composite picture of what the woman you should seek should look like; they also give young women insight in how they ought to construct their lives. Here is a summary list of what a godly woman looks like:

- Physically attractive to you
- Christian who is daily obeying the teachings of Jesus
- Has a gentle and quiet spirit
- Dignified; carries herself well
- High self-esteem (confidence in Christ without arrogance)
- Even tempered
- Faithful to God and her family

- Respectful
- No addictions
- Restrained
- Able to be led
- Protects her heart

Other Things to Consider

The Bible points to fantastic guidelines of what to look for in people we date. There are indicators in life that would be wise to look at, as well. When dating, you should look at a person's family background and evaluate how similar or dissimilar it is to your own. Does he or she come from a background of affluence or poverty, and how will that affect expectations in marriage? What does the parents'

> *People who come from divorced homes are at least 40 percent more likely to get divorced than if their homes weren't broken.*

relationship look like? Is there divorce or infidelity in the family? Is that different than your family? It is a staggering fact that people who come from divorced homes are at least 40 percent more likely to get divorced. If the parents married others after divorcing, the children in those homes are 91 percent more likely to get divorced.[49] This doesn't mean you can't marry someone from a divorced home, nor is it saying if you come from a divorced home, you can't build a successful marriage. It is, however, a strong word of caution that there will be more to overcome in marriage than if you and/or your spouse came from a home that was intact. Remember, you need to be aware of where the pitfalls will be in marriage in order to best defend against them.

You should also observe whether there is bickering or harmony in the home. Is the family going to meddle? Will the parents try to interfere in your relationship by questioning your decisions or will they support you in your new home? If the person you date

---

[49] Source: Nicholas Wolfinger, Understanding the Divorce Cycle, Cambridge University Press, 2005.

has siblings that are married, you can look to them as a guide to how the marriage will be received. When you sit down at a meal at your potential in-laws' table, is it an enjoyable experience? Is your family going to be the one that causes conflict, or will theirs? All of these questions are important to ask now, because when you get married, you also marry your fiancée's family. See how they spend their money and if they are responsible with it. See if they are high maintenance, meaning they take more than you would be willing to provide to make them happy. Look at their political persuasions – it is not impossible, but definitely difficult to be married to someone on the other side of the political aisle because that usually speaks directly to your world view.

Consider taking a good look at the friends of the person you date to see if they encourage or discourage her walk with the Lord. Remember that bad company ruins good morals.[50] If you want the one you are dating to continue in her walk with the Lord, make sure she is surrounded by people who are like minded.

---

[50] 1 Corinthians 15:33

You can tell so much about a person by the choices she has already made about her circle of friends. If she enjoys being wild and crazy, she will want friends that support her in that pursuit. If she wants to pursue godliness, she will try to assemble at least a small circle of friends who will be mutually supportive. Like other areas of her life, you cannot expect she will be enjoying one mode of living today, and scrap all of that for you, once married. It is hard for a leopard to change its spots. The same is true with chosen paths of pursuit and performance. None of these on their own is a deal breaker, but you must consider and evaluate these issues. They can change your perspective on the long term picture of marriage.

Last, but not least, seek wise counsel from Christians that know you well. Over the years, my wife and I have listened to many unhappy couples who jumped into marriage too quickly, didn't listen to or seek sound advice from

> *Seek wise counsel from Christians that know you well.*

friends and family, later confessing that they didn't see or deliberately ignore what others tried to warn them about. The way of a fool is right in his own eyes, but a wise man is he who listens to counsel.[51] Where there is no guidance the people fall, but in abundance of counselors there is victory.[52] Find someone that you trust and ask them if the person you are dating seems right for you. Give them a chance to meet the person and see the two of you interact. One of my mentors was a professor at the dental school I attended. He and I met weekly, outside of class to discuss life and I would pick his brain on everything from marriage to raising children. When my future wife Amanda would visit, I took her along to meet him and his wife and get their input, because I knew that I could trust their judgment. Even after marriage, they were a fantastic resource for us, helping us see things we wouldn't have seen otherwise. If your parents have been good counselors for you in the past, and you have generally respected their opinions and counsel, this would be a

---

[51] Proverbs 12:15
[52] Proverbs 11:14

great time to seek their counsel again. No one knows you more thoroughly than your parents. Introduce him or her to them, and let them get to know the person to see if they complement you.

There is one last thing that is purposely omitted in both lists, and that is the requirement of virginity. God's first plan is that both you and your spouse are virgins when you marry. That is God's design to start your marriage on the best foundation. Certainly, you should consider their sexual history and determine if their past is going to be something you can live with. However, remember, there are some incredible Christian men and women who have stumbled in this area and have gone on to make a powerful impact in God's kingdom. We ought not to identify others, or ourselves for that matter, by our past sin, but rather by how we live for Christ today and our assessment of where they are headed in the future.

Showing Interest (Flirting)

Flirting can be one of the most perplexing forms of non-verbal communication. From personal experience and many discussions with college

> *Ladies, never underestimate the power of your laugh and smile.*

students on this subject, both guys and girls are completely oblivious as to what flirting means to the opposite sex. I have heard the words, "I thought they were into me" more times than I can remember. A prime example is laughter. A girl who laughs at a guy's joking is always the first thing guys list as flirting. Ladies, never underestimate the power of your laugh and smile. Guys perceive your laughter at their jokes and crazy things they do to impress you as flirting, or you being "into" them.

Perhaps you are thinking, "Some guys are just funny," and I would agree. But if you get the feeling a guy is interested in you, and it isn't mutual, be wary of your laughter… it could lead him on. Men are captivated by the laughter of a woman – I would do anything to hear my wife laugh – for some reason it makes me feel valuable. Another thing guys think of as flirting is when girls "touch their neck or play with their [own] hair." When my wife and I had just started dating I can vividly remember late one night we were having a long conversation and she was playing with her hair. I thought, "Wow, this girl is in to me," only to find out later that she always plays with her hair when she is tired. So, apparently, instead of being impressed by my conversational skills, she was just tired!

The classic example when girls think you are flirting is your presence. Here is what I mean by that: If you are always hanging around a girl because you enjoy her company or she is fun to be around, but you have no romantic intentions, that confuses her. Girls often say it "plays games with their minds." To her, you want to be around her because you are interested in her romantically, and if that is the case, keep it up. If not, remove yourself from her world as much as possible. Eye contact is also huge for both guys and girls. An old adage states, "The eyes are the window to the soul." That is exactly what happens when you make prolonged eye contact with someone; if there is interest, your eyes usually meet again. Let that be a reminder. If you aren't interested in someone, don't give them your eyes. Bounce your eyes away. If you are talking to someone and you want to be sure they know that you aren't interested in them romantically, look away frequently, without being rude.

Obviously, if you want to get to know each other better, just being in the same location is a great place to start. Like Ruth did with Boaz, just be present. Place yourself in his or her world… without stalking. If she works at the library, maybe you could read a book in her section. If he works at a coffee shop, maybe you could go have a coffee or an overpriced bottled water. You can never know what

> *If you constantly hang around a girl, and don't have romantic intentions, it will play games with her mind.*

someone is really like until you are around him or her, so that's a great place to start. Flirting isn't wrong… it is a totally natural form of non-verbal communication. Just be sure that you are sending the right signals for the right reasons.

Take Home Points:

- *Get to know people in group settings before jumping into a dating relationship.*

- *Look for someone who isn't just a "Christian" but one with a vibrant walk, actively obeying the teachings of Jesus.*

- *Look to the Bible for the requirements of what to look for in your future spouse.*

- *Examine their family situation – you don't just marry them, you also marry their family.*

- *See what their friends are like – those that pursue godliness will have friends that support them in that endeavor.*

- *Seek wise counsel from Christians that know you well.*

- *Flirting can mean different things to both sexes. Be sure you are sending the right signals.*

Chapter 4: The Dating Relationship

*The mind of man plans his way, but the
LORD directs his steps.
Proverbs 16:9*

࿊

Thus far, we have discussed how dating is like an interview. We have explored the benefits and effects of guarding our hearts, by praying for our future spouse and setting correct priorities in our lives. We discussed how to evaluate people that you date and what requirements God says to look for in them. Now we need to look at how these principles and ideas apply in the dating relationship.

Asking is the Man's Job

Here is a question that we have often received. Can a girl ask a guy out on a date? This is an argument that has continued for a long time. The answer of course is, yes. A woman *can* ask a guy out on a date. The real question is, *should* a girl ask a guy out on a date?

People often point to Ruth in the Bible as evidence that a woman can take the lead in initiating relationship. In doing so, they overlook the bigger picture. Naomi and her Moabite daughter-in-law Ruth had moved back to Bethlehem from Moab after Naomi's husband and son (Ruth's husband) died. As was customary at the time, Ruth went out to pick grain from some nearby fields. By God's design, the field she was in happened to belong to Boaz, a close relative of Naomi's and a kinsman redeemer (according to custom, the closest male relative would marry the widow of the deceased relative

> *Men should initiate and women should respond.*

so that he would not go without children). Boaz, after hearing of Ruth's loyalty to her widowed mother-in-law, showed kindness to her and protected her. When Naomi found this out, she told Ruth to dress herself up. Naomi, confident in Boaz's integrity and the ability of God to govern his reaction, comes up with a plan, gets Ruth dressed up, and sends her off. It was the time of the barley harvest and Boaz was working hard all day, separating and preparing the grain. At the end of the day, when he had eaten and was relaxed, the narrator paints a picture of a contented man at peace. He falls fast asleep under the stars in the warm late-spring evening, outside by the big heap of grain. Once everyone was asleep, Ruth goes over to him, uncovers his feet and lays down beside him. Sometime in the coolness of the night, Boaz caught a chill and awoke to find Ruth there by his bedside. Either because of the darkness, his sleepiness, or because he had never seen Ruth all dolled-up, he didn't recognize her and had to ask her who she was. Ruth, while identifying herself, asks Boaz to redeem her, not out of the blue, but according to the customs of Israel. Given the moral decline during the period of judges which they were in, an average Israelite might have welcomed the night visit of a woman, interpreting her presence as an offer of sexual favors, but not Boaz. He continues to care for her and protect her, navigating the legal system of the day to do so. Once married they have a child, who would be the grandfather of David, the greatest of all the kings of Israel, in the lineage of Jesus. We see from this account the hidden hand of God guiding not only the actions of individuals but their reactions and dispositions, so that in the end God's agenda is accomplished.

It was Boaz who first noticed Ruth and began caring for her – before she knew he could redeem her. He took steps to care for a grieving widow in her time of need. Ruth rightfully asked for Boaz to redeem her according to custom. This historical account is a picture of what Jesus has done

> *Boaz pursued Ruth first, who in turn responded by asking for him to redeem her.*

for us. He pursued us first. He first loved us by taking on our sin. [53] When we confess Jesus as Lord and believe in our hearts that He died for us, Jesus redeems us, just as Boaz redeemed Ruth. [54] That is a far cry from asking a guy out on a date. Ladies, the one thing that you can learn here is that if you are interested in a guy, and he doesn't know you exist – either because he is busy or otherwise preoccupied – hang around and drop hints. This is a very useful teaching extracted from Ruth. Let him know you are there, in appropriate, not brazen, ways. Then, like Ruth, watch to see god at work, and observe the quality and character of the guy you think is worth your interest. Let's think back to previous chapters. Ladies should already be looking for a guy who consistently lives out Christ's principles and who can lead them. If after he knows you are interested in him, he can't lead in something as simple as asking you out on a date, you shouldn't expect him to lead spiritually in the rest of the relationship. Secondly, you might be asking for trouble. If he

---

[53] 1 John 4:13; Ephesians 2:4-9

[54] Romans 10:9; Galatians 4:4-7, Colossians 1:13-14; Hebrews 9:11-12

doesn't like you enough to pursue the relationship, why would you want to go out on a date with him?

In the Bible, there are different roles assigned to men and women. Leadership is the role that is assigned to men; this is true in the church and in the family. Just because men are placed in a position of leadership, doesn't mean that males are superior or that they have innately greater importance in God's kingdom than women (see Esther, Ruth and Mary, for example). It is simply God's design and assignment of the roles between two spiritually equal beings. With the understanding that dating is an interview for marriage, together with the understanding that leadership in the home, according to 1 Corinthians 11 and Ephesians 5, is assigned to men, it is a wise practice to set yourself up with habits that will enable your marriage, not hinder it. As a reminder, under no circumstances are women commanded to submit to men in any relationship other than marriage. That doesn't mean you can't show interest, like hinting around to his friends that you are interested. However, if the guy is still oblivious to your interest in him, don't "grab the reins" and take over leadership in his role as the initiator. That is the same temptation that can happen once married, and it is best to learn to deal with it now. What you can do is pray, "God, if this guy is the one for me, would you please wake him up!" You can pray and see God operate on your behalf. Remember Ruth did everything that she could do with a clear conscience and a pure reputation… then she waited for God to do what only He could. God is sovereign, and your identity is as a daughter of the risen Lord, not as any man's girlfriend. Be content where you are, and wait for the man to make the move. If it doesn't work out, it is probably because it wasn't supposed to. So in dating, men should initiate and women should respond. Men should take the leadership role in asking the girl out, giving the woman the opportunity to respond.

Be Candid with Your Intentions

> *Be open and up-front about your intentions.*

After getting to know a girl from a far and hanging out with her through group activities, I tell guys who want to know how to pursue a girl to be open about their intentions. Never make a woman guess where she stands. Being up front is one of the best ways to guard both of your hearts, and the first step is asking her out on a date. So, whether this means that you approach the girl directly (or perhaps her father), you, gentlemen, need to initiate. This isn't something that should be done in a text message or via whatever social media is current – girls consistently say that they hate it when guys ask them out this way, so take note.

> *Avoid asking a girl out using text messages.*

Guys, I know this can be hard for some of you, but when you ask a girl out you have to use the word "date"! You can't ask her for coffee, or lunch, or to go study or any other thing you can think of to avoid saying the word because you are afraid of rejection. Ask her out on a D-A-T-E, date. That word is loaded with meaning and expectations. It means that there is intention behind the time together. It means that you think highly enough of her to pursue her romantically. It also means that if you go to a place to eat or to the movies, the man pays. Let me say that more bluntly… the guy picks up the tab for everything on the date. When guys don't pay, it sends mixed messages to the girl about his intentions, and the guy often doesn't get a second chance. Ask any Christian friend who is a girl, she will likely tell you if the guy doesn't pay, it is not a date. The biggest complaint I hear from girls is that guys aren't clear with their intentions. Often times they phrase it as "mind games." Obviously Jedi mind tricks aren't at play here (although that would be awesome), so what are they talking about? As discussed previously, if you take a girl out for lunch or coffee, especially if it is on a regular basis, and you haven't clearly defined that your intention is either to pursue her romantically or just to hang out as friends, it will cause her to constantly wonder what the point of the relationship is. Girls need to know where they stand.

Just as it is the guy's role to initiate in the dating relationship, it is the girl's role to respond, whether positively or negatively. Ladies, there is no way to say this without sounding cheesy or melodramatic. Men have fought in battles, driven race cars at crazy speeds, climbed impossible mountains, and built empires - all to prove their worth and manhood. A woman is the only being in the universe that holds the immense power to strip men of all dignity, pride, and honor with just a few words. When guys ask you out on a date, in their minds they are putting their pride on the line, with fear and trepidation. So if you want men to lead, you must be mindful of how much power you wield when they pose that question to you. If you aren't interested in them, you shouldn't say yes just

> *Girls need to know where they stand.*

because you feel sorry for them, but you also shouldn't slam the preverbal door in their face either. Remember, God tells us to speak the truth in

If she really is worth pursuing then go get her!

love.[55] Ladies, if you aren't interested, here is a great way to say that lovingly, "Thank you so much for taking the initiative to actually ask me out on a date. I'm flattered and respect you so much for that, but I don't see us being more than just friends." To be sure, he will still be let down, but when done gently, it is an incredible help to him the next time he asks a woman out, because he won't have the memory of a horrible rejection lingering in his mind for the enemy to replay over and over.

Gentlemen, if she says yes, remember it is an interview, and that interview goes both ways. When you pick her up, don't sit in your truck and honk your horn waiting for her to come out – ever. Believe me, I've seen it happen, and it speaks volumes to the girl.

---

[55] Ephesians 4:15

Walk up to her door and go get her… remember you are *pursuing* her. If she really is worth pursuing then go get her!

This should go without saying, but when you are on the date, TALK! Both of you should ask lots of questions. Try to get the other person talking about anything and everything; that's how you learn about each other. I have a friend who got a book filled with crazy, random questions and would pick a few for each date like, "If you had to die one of two ways, by being burned alive or by drowning, which one would you take?" Like I said, crazy and random, but it gets the conversation moving when there is a lull, and you learn things about people that you never would have before. If you aren't particularly gifted at conversation, pick up a book about it. Make an effort to pursue by learning about her interests, who she is, where she came from and where she wants to be in the future.

End of the Night

So you have been on the date. The guy initiated, and the girl responded. He paid, and you both had an enjoyable time

Be intentional, it may be awkward, but she will respect you for it.

(or perhaps, a not-so-enjoyable time). Now it is time for the date to end. Unless I'm missing something, there is no parable in the Bible where Jesus looks at the twelve disciples and explains in detail the right way to take their dates home. So, using what we have already learned, there are some solid principles on which we can develop our own patterns of behavior. First and foremost, guys, walk the girl to the door. Don't just drop her off at the corner of her street, no matter how badly the date went. Remember to be open and honest with each other. Guys, you should initiate the conversation on the way to the door about how you thought the date went. Be intentional; it may be awkward, but she will respect you for it.

If things went well, you can say, "I had a great

> *Never keep her guessing.*

time with you tonight, and I would love the opportunity to get to see you again. Can I call you tomorrow after five?" Then if she says yes, call her the next day, following up on your request and letting her know you can be trusted. If things didn't go well, you will need to be a bit more delicate. As you walk her to the door you can say something like, "I don't want to lead you on in any way. It seems to me that, while we had a nice time, we probably are not going to benefit from continuing this dating relationship. What do you think?" Ladies, if he hasn't taken the lead, and you think things have gone poorly, use the same line. This is a way that you can respectfully tell him that there won't be another date, while honoring his opinion and still allowing him to "save face." Always give the other person an easy out. You are giving them the opportunity to agree and move on. Men should always be clear about their intentions are and the nature of the relationship. Never keep her guessing. Great leaders point the direction and give vision. It can feel risky and vulnerable, but it is your job – own it.

The most important thing that both of you must keep in mind is that you need to guard your heart first, and the heart of the person you are dating second. Rejection can be painful, but if you keep in mind that you are dating to find your spouse, the faster you come to the conclusion that the person you are dating isn't "the one" and the faster you get out of the dating relationship, the faster you can get on to the business of finding your mate.

One last point should be discussed – How to say goodnight. If things go well and both of you enjoy each other's company, that last few moments of time you have together have the potential to set the tone, good or bad, for the rest of your dating relationship in the physical realm. When you say goodnight, turn around and go home. Don't kiss, don't go into her apartment, don't linger, just say goodnight and "ride off into the sunset." If you follow this principle you will set yourself up for success in the rest of your dating relationship. In summary: guys ask (in person), use the word date, the guy pays for the date, the guy should make his intentions and nature of the relationship known, and both guys and girls should be active in guarding each other's hearts.

Keep Intentions on the Front Burner

> *Make your intentions known early and often.*

So you've successfully strung a series of great dates together. You are enjoying each other's company and everything seems to be going great…

now we need to talk about the three words that strike fear into the bravest of souls. I'm not talking about the words "I love you" - we'll deal with that in the next chapter. I'm talking about the "DTR" – defining the relationship. Remember, we learned that we are to watch over our hearts with all diligence, for from them flow the springs of life.[56] It is all about guarding our hearts. There can be a great deal of anxiety and fear

---

[56] Proverbs 4:23

when approaching this conversation. The fear comes directly from the fear of rejection. None of us wants to be rejected – especially by someone whom we are really into –

> *Rejection, while it might hurt initially, should remind you that you are one step closer to finding the right guy or girl.*

but if we are to consistently guard our hearts, we need to be intentional and fearless in doing so. Rejection, while it might hurt initially, should remind us that we are one step closer to finding the right guy or girl…elsewhere.

At this point, which is early in the dating relationship, you don't need to have a long discussion about how many kids you want to have and where you want to live when you are married. You do, however, need to make your intentions for dating known early and often. Guys should be especially intentional of leading in this area because it has a tremendous protective mechanism for both people in the relationship. However, if the guy in the relationship hasn't done so, the girl should take initiative and ask him his intentions. The conversation doesn't have to be a big ordeal. In fact, it is best if it isn't. You can say:

> *I have been having a great time with you. I want you to know that, while I am not looking to get married in the next few weeks, I think the point of dating is to find the one we are supposed to marry. You have all of the qualities I look for in someone I would like to be with. With that said, you have my word if that ever changes I will come to you personally and tell you. Please, if you ever feel that we aren't meant to be together, please tell me so that we don't put ourselves in more temptation than is necessary. May we have this conversation again in the near future?*

By phrasing it that way, you accomplish multiple objectives. You bring up the fact that the point of dating is to find the person you want to marry. If this scares them off, it is a good thing! You don't want to date someone who doesn't share the same "big picture" as you do! Secondly, not only do you give your word that you will be up front about your feelings, you give permission to break up with you. That is incredibly important. It shows confidence on your part and empowers the person you are dating to be open with their feelings without worrying about hurting you. Lastly, you get permission to talk about your relationship again within an agreed upon time. This makes it much easier to broach the topic again for both of you because you both know it is coming, and you don't have to wonder when it will take place.

The Big One

This is the point where palms start to sweat. You have been dating awhile and it is time to find out where the both of you are and where you would both like to be. The question I get asked is, "When is the "Big DTR" appropriate?" The answer is different for everyone. When my wife and I started dating, it was in the fall of my senior year in college. She was a year behind me. I had just been accepted to dental school and she was in the process of applying to vet school; both of which are four year commitments before residency. That wouldn't have been a big deal, except there was no dental school near a vet school in the state of Texas. Naturally, both of us were planning on going to school in-state. I felt that, for me personally, it would be unwise to have a four year, long-distance dating relationship that would ultimately cause emotional turmoil and definite prolonged temptation (not that it can't be done, I just knew that I shouldn't, and I also rested in the knowledge that if she really was who God wanted me to marry, she would still be there). So, within the first three weeks, I sat down with her and had an open conversation about where we were headed. You read that right, three weeks. Even I thought that I was crazy! That's not to say every dating relationship should have a big DTR that early, but I knew that if I stayed in this relationship without addressing the obvious difficulties ahead, we could be headed for trouble, and me for heartache. To my surprise, she appreciated my honesty and desire to guard our hearts, and we both agreed to pray about it. Over the next few months God made it clear to her, even after getting accepted to vet school that He wanted her to go into law. Conveniently, there is a law school near every dental school in Texas, and the rest is history.

Obviously for you, the right time to have the "Big DTR" probably won't be in the first few weeks of dating. I want you to remember, however, to make your intentions known early and often. I tell guys, and girls, that within the first few months, and every few months thereafter, to have some sort of discussion about where they are relationally (say every three months or quarterly). Again, guys should lead in this. Girls, however, still need

> *Leading in dating means that when you part ways that person is closer to Jesus than they were before you met.*

to be active in guarding their hearts. If the guy is unwilling, the girl should broach the topic. As a reminder, girls should always be wary of a man who is unwilling to lead.

I don't think there is a right or wrong way to have a DTR, but there are some definite high points you should hit in your discussion. Revisit the purpose of dating (to find your spouse). Talk about spiritual leadership. Leading in dating means leaving the person closer to Jesus than before you met. Have an open conversation about physical temptation and promise not to lead each other into it. Both of you should pray that if you aren't right for each other, it would be clear to you both. Promise that if there is a time that you don't think that you are right for each other, you will respectfully break up and not lead them on. Finally, ask permission to have this discussion again in an agreed upon time. If having this conversation causes the end of a relationship, the person probably isn't your future spouse, and it is a good thing. It only keeps you from temptation and leading on someone else.

How Long to Date before Marriage

If you ask Christian leaders across the globe this question, you will probably get as many answers as people you ask. There are some phenomenal

> *Hearts have a tendency to getting caught up in the emotion of the moment. Minds have a way of tempering that emotion.*

people that have gotten married after only a few weeks of dating and have been married fifty years. A friend of mine met his wife in high school, and at the ages of 18 and 19, right after graduation, got married and went on a honeymoon to Six Flags. They are still going strong after more than 35 years. There are people that have dated for years before getting married just to "be sure," whose marriages have failed. In all things, you need to ask God with an open and sincere heart when the timing is right; He won't let you down.

Paul tells us one of the ways God will speak to us when he says:

> *Be anxious for nothing, but in everything by prayer and supplication with thanksgiving let your requests be made known to God. And the peace of God, which surpasses all comprehension, will guard your hearts and your minds in Christ Jesus.*[57]

That verse is important. First, it tells us not to fret over the decision, but trust that God will provide an answer through prayer. Second, it tells us how we can expect that answer – peace in both our hearts and our minds. It is imperative that peace be in both your heart *and* your mind. Hearts have a tendency to get caught up in the emotion of the moment. Minds have a way of tempering that emotion. Likewise, if you think a person is good for you, but don't feel it in your heart, that is a definite negative. When the right one comes along, and you have spent time in prayer, there will be a supernatural peace in both your heart and your mind. Of course, the opposite is true as well. If that person

---

[57] Philippians 4:6

isn't right for you, God will give you a supernatural unrest in either your heart or your mind telling you to get out.

I would say that a good rule of thumb in dating for marriage is to try to see the person through all four seasons. And by seasons, I mean literally summer, fall, winter and spring. If you date a person for at least a year, you will get the opportunity to see how their family celebrates all the holidays, how they spend time during the summer and winter, and how they interact with each other over the long haul. Remember this: it is hard to fake it for a year. It would be devastating to make lifelong decisions based on only a few months' worth of information, only to find out that the people weren't being truthful or were just acting that way for show. I have a dear friend that married quickly, only to find out that the woman he fell in love with, and her family, were all alcoholics who were experts in hiding their addiction. That marriage ultimately ended in divorce.

How to Break Up Respectfully

Breaking up stinks, no matter how it is done and how kind and effective your words are. That is why so many songs are written about it! Any time you have invested time and emotion in a relationship and then see that relationship come to an end, it is difficult. However, if you have already been dating with the principles outlined previously – being open about your intentions and having a "DTR" regularly that includes asking permission to break up with the person if you find out that he or she isn't the one – it will be much easier, when the time comes. During your regular DTR's you would have discussed breaking up and the reasons for doing so. We need to try to be respectful without being hurtful. Go to the other person and say something like this:

> *I told you from the beginning that I would protect our hearts first and foremost and that if at any point in time I feel that we aren't right for each other, I would tell you, and we would*

> *part ways so that we wouldn't fall into*
> *undue temptation. With that being said,*
> *I don't see us being life-long partners,*
> *and I don't want to drag this out further*
> *and cause either of us to stumble.*

Now, while being far from easy, that is still better than the old "let's just be friends" speech, the "it's not you it's me" line, or my personal non-favorite, "God told me to break up with you." Remember, part of guarding your heart and the hearts of those you date is not damaging their heart in any way. You want to break up in a way that they know it is over, without injuring them emotionally.

Take Home Points:

- *Men should initiate, women should respond.*

- *It is the guy's job to ask the girl out on a date.*

- *When asking a girl out, use the word "date," it lets the girl know what you want from the relationship.*

- *Always ask the girl out in person, face to face, or over the phone where she can hear your voice. Using text messages or social media to ask a girl out on a date should be avoided.*

- *Be open with your intentions for the relationship from the very beginning.*

- *Let the person know how you thought the date went as you walk to the door at the end of the evening so they won't have to guess what you are thinking.*

- *Keep your intentions on the front burner. Define the relationship early and often.*

- *Continue dating until you know whether they are the right one and take appropriate, timely action either through proposal or breakup.*

Chapter 5: How Love Works

*Nevertheless, each individual among you also is
to love his own wife even as himself, and the
wife must see to it that she respects her
husband.*
Ephesians 5:33

❧❧

The Meaning of Love

Often, we hear about love at first sight. Two
people "find each other" and fall madly in love – as if
love involved angry people falling into a ditch. The
problem with understanding love *only* as a feeling is
that if we can fall in love, we can also fall out of love,
because feelings change – just as I feel hungry one
moment, I won't the next. We also hear, especially in

> *Love is more than just a feeling, but also more than a choice.*

the church, that love is a choice; that we choose to love others. However, love is also not *only* a choice made without emotion. The point is made clearer when thinking about the opposite of love, which is hate. Hate is most definitely a choice, but there is most certainly a feeling associated with hate. The issue with understanding love only as a choice has the tendency to make our mind the decisive moral agent, disengaging the heart, and unintentionally degrading the importance of loving feelings. Therefore, if love is only a choice, there is a duty to perform… not very romantic. There is a very specific interplay, between the feeling of love, and the choice to love that we need to understand.

Let us first separate out love from attraction. When we first meet someone and "fall head over heels," that feeling of attraction is infatuation combined with excitement, sexual tension, and fear.

Studies have shown that the neurotransmitter Dopamine is at a higher level in people in this state. Dopamine is instrumental in how our brain perceives pleasure and pain, has been linked to desire and addiction, and can cause euphoria. In fact, this love-struck state has a similar effect as narcotics, like cocaine and morphine, on Dopamine levels in the brain.[58] That sheds new light on the passage in Song of Solomon, where the friends of the bride and groom say to them, "Eat, friends, drink, and be drunk with love!"[59]

When we see that special someone, we get the feeling of "butterflies" in our stomachs. That gut-twisting sensation is the work of the fight-or-flight hormone adrenaline (also called epinephrine) which is released from the adrenal gland, right above our kidneys (in the area of your stomach). It gushes adrenaline like a big wet sponge directly into our

---

[58] Childress, A.R.; Ehrman, R.N.; Wang, Z.; Li, Y.; Sciortino, N.; Hakun, J.; Jens, W.; Suh, J.; Listerud, J.; Marquez, K.; Franklin, T.; Langleben, D.; Detre, J.; O'Brien, C.P. Prelude to passion: limbic activation by "unseen" drug and sexual cues. PLoS ONE 2008; 3(1):e1506.

[59] Song of Solomon 5:1

veins, in the same way as when we are frightened. Adrenaline courses through the blood stream causing our hearts to race, our palms to sweat and become shaky, our mouth to go dry and we become more alert, all at the instant we catch a glimpse of the person we are attracted to. This biochemical response is quite a rush and mostly enjoyable – the problem is, like with most other chemical highs, it eventually goes away. That "love-struck" feeling is just that, a feeling brought about by a biochemical reaction of our bodies. Most often, when you ask someone to define love, they usually speak in terms of that moment. Most great novels and plays focus on this moment and these huge emotions. We like reading these kinds of books, because we hope that someday we might have the same exciting response to someone. Unfortunately, many of these great books and plays don't point to the necessary supplemental love and work that is required to sustain a loving relationship beyond this first powerful attraction. But that isn't all there is to love – it's only the initial attraction phase. This phase is not unimportant, but its exciting beginning elements are not the ones that sustain love.

Love is not just a feeling, but love is also not just a choice. Love is feeling and choice. Love is emotion

That "love-struck" feeling is just that, a feeling brought about by a biochemical reaction of our bodies.

and action. To better understand this, let's look at the words God used for love in the Bible. In the Old Testament, written in Hebrew, there are three main words used for love between humans: Rea (pronounced rie-ah), Ahaba (pronounced ahah-vah) and Dod (pronounced doh-d). Rea is a word primarily used for the love of a friend or companion; this is the friend who you share ideas, experiences, hopes and dreams with. When Hushai goes back into Jerusalem as double agent to spy on Absolam for David, the word "rea" is used for his friendship with David.[60]

Ahaba is the next step; this word encompasses all of the word Rea and puts with it commitment and

---

[60] 2 Samuel 15:37

unconditional love. Ahaba has connection; it is desire mixed with decision. Ahaba says I know everything about you – the good and the bad – and I'm still committed to you. It is interesting that this is the word used when God says, "You shall love the LORD your God with all your heart and with all your soul and with all your might."[61] Not only is the word "ahaba" used for love, it is almost as if the picture of the word is repeated in the last "with all your heart and with all your soul and with all your might." Another time ahaba is used is where the Bible says after the young David defeated Goliath, the soul of Jonathan was knit to the soul of David, and Jonathan loved him as himself.[62] There was a commitment in that friendship that isn't in normal, everyday friendships; it was one that lasted through Jonathan's father (Saul) trying to kill David, and Jonathan basically giving up his birthright to the throne to David, God's chosen king. The Bible puts the two words together and illustrates beautifully the relationship between rea and ahaba:

---

[61] Deuteronomy 6:5
[62] 1 Samuel 18:1

> *A man of too many friends comes to*
> *ruin, but there is a friend who sticks*
> *closer than a brother.*[63]

To rephrase using the specific Hebrew words, "A man of too many *rea* comes to ruin, but there is an *ahaba* who sticks closer than a brother." Where rea is much more casual, ahaba is closer than family.

Even closer still is the word "dod." When rea and ahaba are present in a relationship between a husband and a wife, dod comes in, which literally refers to sexual intimacy; this is the passion and the romantic feelings, the physical, sexual part. In Song of Solomon, the groom says to his bride:

> *How beautiful is your love, my sister,*
> *my bride! How much better is your love*
> *than wine, and the fragrance of your*
> *oils than all kinds of spices!*[64]

---

[63] Proverbs 18:24
[64] Song of Solomon 4:10

Putting it in modern day English he says, "How awesome it is to have sex with you! It's the best!" That's a man who's taken by his new bride! Any newlywed would surely put it in similar terms. The bride uses both dod and ahaba where she says, "I adjure you, O daughters of Jerusalem, if you find my beloved, as to what you will tell him: for I am lovesick."[65] We see how these two aspects of love work in a marriage relationship through the words of the young bride, dearly missing her husband, asking her friends that, "if you see my lover" (literally my "dodi"), "tell him that I am sick with 'ahaba'."

In the New Testament, which was written in Greek, there are mainly two words used: agape and phileo. Interestingly, "eros," the Greek term for sexual love, is not used in the New Testament. Agape is always the word used in the New Testament to describe God's love for us. We often hear that agape love is "unconditional love," which is absolutely true, but it is also so much more. Agape is always concerned with showing others that they are valued, at all costs.

---

[65] Song of Solomon 5:8

Let's look at how agape is applied in 1 Corinthians chapter 13, where Paul always uses the word "agape" for love.

If I speak with the tongues of men and of angels, but do not have love, I have become a noisy gong or a clanging cymbal. If I have the gift of prophecy, and know all mysteries and all knowledge; and if I have all faith, so as to remove mountains, but do not have love, I am nothing. And if I give all my possessions to feed the poor, and if I surrender my body to be burned, but do not have love, it profits me nothing. Love is patient, love is kind and is not jealous; love does not brag and is not arrogant, does not act unbecomingly; it does not seek its own, is not provoked, does not take into account a wrong suffered, does not rejoice in unrighteousness, but rejoices with the truth; bears all things, believes all things, hopes all things, endures all things. Love never fails; but if there are gifts of prophecy, they will be done away; if there are tongues, they will cease; if there is knowledge, it will be done away. For we know in part and we prophesy in part; but when the perfect comes, the partial will be done away. When I was a child, I used to speak like a child, think like a child, reason like a child; when I became a man, I did away with childish things. For now we see in a mirror dimly, but then face to face; now I know in part, but then I will know fully just as I also have been fully known. But now faith, hope, love, abide these three; but the greatest of these is love.

This chapter in 1 Corinthians shows us how limitless agape really is. If we are valued by another above all else, as agape love calls for, the qualities described here is what we will experience. Agape love is one that is always concerned

> *Agape is always concerned with showing others that they are valued, at all costs.*

with showing another that they are valued at all costs, not for the sake of showing value, but because of how much they mean to you. The focus is on the one to whom agape love is being shown. That is the point of John 3:16:

> *"For God so loved the world, that He gave His only begotten Son, that whoever believes in Him shall not perish, but have eternal life."*

God valued us so much, that He would give up His own Son in order to pay the debt of our sin and get us back from the grips of hell. That statement completely encompasses the "value at all costs" attitude of agape.

Phileo is another word used for love in the New Testament. The root word, philos, is translated "friend," and a variant "philema" refers to a kiss of greeting. Phileo means to have affection for, to earnestly like, or to feel a kinship with. In other words, phileo is the "feeling" of love. When Lazarus became ill and died, Jesus wept bitterly for His friend. The grief was so visible, according to John, those around Him used the word phileo saying, "See how He loved him!"[66] He felt love toward Lazarus. In the negative sense, Jesus says of the scribes that they "love" (using the word phileo) the attention that their status brought them.[67] They were more in love with their position in life than they were with their God; so to the scribes, their position was their god.

---

[66] John 11:35-36
[67] Luke 20:46

The interplay between phileo and agape can be seen where agape is translated "love" and philos is "friend" where Jesus says,

> *If we show others that we truly value them, they will feel love towards us.*

"Greater love has no one than this, that one lay down his life for his friends."[68] You can't show value to those that you feel love for in a greater way than to die for them. That is the meaning behind Paul's statement, "Husbands, love your wives, just as Christ also loved the church and gave Himself up for her."[69] Husbands are to show their wives value in such a powerful way that their wives know they would die for them. If we make a conscious effort to truly show others that we value them (agape-love), they will inherently feel love (phileo) toward us. Likewise, if others show that they truly value us (agape), we will feel love (phileo) toward them. That is how the interplay between

---

[68] John 15:13
[69] Ephesians 5:25

"choosing love" and "feeling love" works.

Men and Women are Different

> *We are different from our DNA to how we perceive love.*

There is nothing ground-breaking in the statement, "men and women are different," but the important and fundamental concept is often forgotten. I'm not merely talking about seventh grade biology class here. From our DNA to how we perceive love – we are different. Having a greater understanding of our differences can bring greater acceptance and love between men and women. Men and women differ on even the cellular level because they carry a differing chromosomal patterns; the implications of our genetic makeup range from the obvious to the extremely subtle. Dr. Paul Popenoe, founder of the American Institute of Family Relations in Los Angeles, dedicated most of his working life to the research of biological differences between the sexes. From his research, he found that females outlive males by four to eight years because of their greater constitutional vitality and perhaps because of their unique chromosomal makeup. Women's thyroid glands are larger and more active than that of men, giving them a greater resistance to cold. Women's blood contains more water and twenty percent fewer red cells. Since the red cells supply oxygen to the body's cells, women in general tire more easily. An illustration of this is that when the working day in British factories was increased from ten to twelve hours during wartime conditions, accidents increased 150 percent among women, but for men, not at all. [70]

Dr. Willard Harley, a clinical psychologist and marriage counselor, wrote a book titled *His Needs, Her Needs: Building an Affair-Proof Marriage*, and in it he lists the most common needs for both men and women, as seen in his counseling over the years. Dr. Harley found that the top five needs of women (in no

---

[70] Taken from Dr. Paul Popenoe, "Are Women Really Different?" Family Life. Vol. 31, February 1971.

particular order) are:

- Affection
- Conversation
- Honesty and Openness
- Financial Support
- Family Commitment

For men, he found a different pattern. The top needs of men were consistently (again in no particular order):

- Sexual Fulfillment
- Recreational Companionship
- Physical Attractiveness
- Domestic Support
- Admiration (Respect)

Notice that *not one* of the top five needs for men and women are the same! The lists are completely different! Proof of this became more evident to me after I married Amanda. I love to work with my hands by working on cars and building things, and I enjoy it when Amanda helps and hangs out with me while I work. I feel like we have had a great time together conquering the project. However, on multiple occasions, she has ended up frustrated or in tears at the end of the project because we weren't talking face to face. You see, while my need for companionship doing something I love was met, her need for face-to-face conversation was not. It's just the way we were created. Those needs not only affect the way we view marriage, but, to some degree, they color the way the sexes view dating.

The way that men and women feel value (that agape-love) is different, too. Women, primarily, feel valued, or loved, when they feel cherished. Men primarily feel valued when they feel respected. If you were to ask a room full of women, "Would you rather feel loved or respected?" almost every woman will say they would rather feel loved. If you ask a room full of men the same question, almost one hundred percent would say they would rather feel respected. Why is that? The Bible gives us a glimpse into how God created us differently when it comes to love. It says:

> *Nevertheless, each individual among you also is to love his own wife even as himself, and the wife must see to it that she respects her husband.*[71]

Did you know that the Bible never says that women should love their husbands? That's because men don't feel loved that way. Likewise, the Bible never tells men to respect their wives, because that's not how they feel loved. Now I am not saying women don't deserve respect – quite the opposite. Nor am I saying that men don't need to be loved. What I am saying is when women show men value in the language of respect, men will feel loved. If men show women love in their language, by cherishing and loving them (and by the way that will also mean they respect them as well), they will feel loved.

So right about now you may be saying, "Fantastic, what does this have to do with dating?" Ladies, you might wonder, why guys like to spend so much time with each other, and why when they get

---

[71] Ephesians 5:33

together with their best friends, they all of a sudden start talking when they are mostly silent around you. You might wonder why they go crazy and do stupid things when they congregate with each other. One reason, is that they want to try to impress you. But there is still another reason that we can see in 2 Samuel when David learns of the death of his best friend, Johnathan. In grief, David cries out, "I am distressed for you, my brother Jonathan; you have been very pleasant to me. Your love to me was more wonderful than the love of women."[72] Now, we know from the stories of David with his wives and the infamous indiscretion with Bathsheba that he was far from homosexual. The key to this passage is knowing what words were used for love. Ahaba is the Hebrew word used for love, and it was translated into Greek in the Septuagint as "agape." It is easier for men to feel valued by other men because they speak the same

---

[72] 2 Samuel 1:26

> *If you want to show others value, you have to do it the way they understand it.*

language – respect. David is saying that the relationship he had with Johnathan came easier than even the relationship between him and his wife.

Likewise guys, you might have noticed that when girls get together they make crafts with each other and complement one another on their clothes and hair or the décor of their rooms. Seriously, when is the last time you heard a guy doing that with other guys on a consistent basis? It is not how men are wired.

The point is that if you want to show others value, especially those you date, you have to do it in a way they understand. Ladies, you have to be, as Paul says, temperate (which means respectful and not brash) and dignified (which means worthy of respect) in regard to men. [73] Men, you need to aspire, in marriage, to be the man who communicates value through cherishing his woman to the point that she

---

[73] 1 Timothy 3:11

knows he would be willing to lay down his life for her[74], and make sure to honor her so that your prayers won't be hindered.[75]

---

[74] Ephesians 5:25
[75] 1 Peter 3:7

Take Home Points:

- *Love is not the same thing as attraction.*

- *Love is feeling with choice.*

- *Men and women are different in how they perceive love. Men crave respect; women want to be cherished.*

- *If you want to show others value, you have to do it in the way they understand it.*

Chapter 6: The Physical Relationship

I want you to swear, O daughters of Jerusalem,
do not arouse or awaken my love until she
pleases.
Song of Solomon 8:4

అ

Everything we have talked about thus far has dealt with the emotional side of the dating relationship. We stared by looking at what God's Word says about guarding our hearts and ways we can implement that in our lives. We have discussed how to best evaluate prospective candidates for marriage by seeking wisely, looking for qualities that God says are important. We then laid practical principles from which to operate in the dating relationship. While the emotional side of the dating relationship is extremely important and must be handled correctly, we must also look at how the Bible tells us to handle the physical (sexual) side of relationships.

Don't Arouse Love Before It Is Time

The physical relationship always progresses.

It only takes a cursory reading of the Old and New Testaments to realize that sexual sin has plagued men and women since the Garden of Eden. From the time before Noah, through the new church in Corinth and up to today, sexual sin has caused untold pain and spiritual casualties. Let me remind you of what we learned in the chapter "How Love Works." Remember that the word "Rea" is used for a friend or companion and that "Ahaba" is the next step. Ahaba includes all of the word Rea and puts with it commitment and unconditional love. It is desire mixed with decision. In Song of Solomon, the bride begs her friends not to arouse "love" before its time.[76] The word used there is "ahaba." The message is clear. She is saying, "Don't progress beyond friendship into the physical relationship before it is time."

We have to remember that a physical relationship always progresses with very little encouragement on our part. You can think about it like a road that starts at holding hands and ends at sexual intercourse. Once you start down that road, you don't go backwards – it is a one way street. The physical relationship always progresses. You must be sure that you take precautions in your dating relationship to guard against going too far in the physical relationship. Paul says in his letter to the Romans:

> *But put on the Lord Jesus Christ, and make no provision for the flesh in regard to its lusts.*[77]

---

[76] Song of Solomon 8:4, and also in 2:7
[77] Romans 13:14

What this doesn't mean is that you draw a legalistic line, walk right up to it consistently and hang out there. It means if you both know you have struggled in the past, don't be alone in tempting situations. Walking up to the line, and staring at the next step, generally ends up with us wandering on to the other side of the line, and wondering how it happened so quickly. There seems to be flashpoints for everyone. That is, when we reach a certain point in physical intimacy, it is nearly impossible to stop at that point. Our goal in preparing to date is to figure out what our flashpoint is, then step back about two steps from it. For some, it might mean any kind of touching. If you can't do it in a restaurant with everyone watching, it is probably not a good idea to do it at all. Paul says:

> *If you both know you have struggled in the past, don't be alone in tempting situations.*

> For this is the will of God, your
> sanctification; that is, that you abstain

from sexual immorality; that each of you know how to possess his own vessel in sanctification and honor, not in lustful passion, like the Gentiles who do not know God [78]

Guys, you need to remember that in order to be a spiritual leader in a dating relationship, the girls you date should be in a better relationship with Jesus than before you met her – that is the point Paul was making. Sanctification is the process by which we become more like Christ. Being self-controlled, and abstaining from sexual immorality, is a major step towards that goal. Gentlemen, you need to be more interested in the girl's sexual purity, than even she is. In other words, the girl might allow you to take various steps, normally considered foreplay. You might think, "Well, she must have considered it okay, because she let me." Doing this is wrongly abdicating leadership in the relationship to her. Men demonstrate leadership by deciding limits, limits that will preserve both of your

---

[78] 1 Thessalonians 4:3-5

integrities and consciences.

That brings me to another point. The Bible never says, "Don't have sex before marriage." In the same way, the Bible doesn't say, "Don't drive off in someone else's car without permission." That doesn't mean car-jacking is fair game for Christians. The definition of adultery is having sex with someone other than your spouse. You are either married, or you aren't. If you are having sex with someone you are not married to, you are committing adultery. The Bible uses two words in the Greek to define adultery, or sex outside of marriage. The first is "moicheuo," which applies directly to someone who is married having sex with someone other than their spouse.[79] The second, "porneia" (which is where we get the word pornography) is a broader term that applies to all forms of sexual immorality, including sex outside of marriage (often translated specifically as fornication).[80] Just as the principle "You shall not steal"[81] applies to car-jacking, "You shall not commit

---

[79] Mathew 5:27
[80] Matthew 15:19
[81] Exodus 20:15

adultery" applies to sex before marriage.

It has been shown in multiple studies that those who are virgins on their wedding day have a much lower chance of divorce than those who are not. Edward Laumann did a massive and highly respected study, conducted at the University of Chicago. In the study he stated, "For both genders, we find that virgins have dramatically more stable first marriages… those who are virgins at marriage have much lower rates of separation and divorce."[82] He also found, "Those who marry as non-virgins are also more likely – all other things being equal – to be unfaithful over the remainder of their life compared with those spouses who do marry as virgins."[83] So when we follow the principles God has outlined in the Bible, clearly we are protecting our marriages before they even begin.

So the logical next question is, "What if I'm

---

[82] Edward O. Laumann et al., The Social Organization of Sexuality: Sexual Practices in the United States, (Chicago: University of Chicago Press, 1994), p. 503-505.
[83] Edward O. Laumann et al., The Social Organization of Sexuality: Sexual Practices in the United States, (Chicago: University of Chicago Press, 1994), p. 505.

not a virgin?" Let me begin by saying, you are not a lost cause – all have fallen short of the glory of God.[84] The enemy will tell you that you've failed, you're dirty, you're damaged goods, and no Christian will want you as a spouse. That is a lie. When you accepted the sacrifice of Jesus on the Cross, His blood paid for your sin. It was His blood that washed you clean from all the dirt and mud of your sin – past, present and future – white as snow.[85] You aren't broken, you've been made new. You aren't damaged goods, you are a new creation.[86] Your sins were as scarlet and now are as white as snow.[87]

> *There is nothing that can protect your mind or your heart from the memories of premarital sex.*

Having sex before marriage will always have consequences at some point in your life, especially in marriage, which is possibly why

---

[84] Romans 3:23
[85] Isaiah 1:18
[86] 2 Corinthians 5:17
[87] Isaiah 1:18

it can be so damaging. There is nothing that can protect your mind or your heart from the memories of premarital sex. You can never erase the memories of "going too far" with someone else. God promises us, "If we confess our sins, He is faithful and righteous to forgive us our sins and to cleanse us from all unrighteousness."[88] If you have put your faith in Jesus, God has forgiven you. To move on in life, you need to acknowledge that what you did was a sin and repent of that sin. You then have to accept God's forgiveness in your life, which also means accepting freedom from guilt and forgiving yourself. Paul held the coats of those that stoned Stephen to death, all the while approving of their actions.[89] He admits to Timothy his regrets about that day, but he doesn't wallow in self-pity over his past sins.[90] Rather, he forces himself to let go of the past and press forward.[91] The blood of Jesus doesn't just cover our sins, it covers our guilt.[92]

---

[88] 1 John 1:9
[89] Acts 22:19-20
[90] 1 Timothy1:12-15
[91] Philippians 3:13-14
[92] Hebrews 9:14

There is no condemnation in Christ Jesus,[93] and we are a new creation.[94] It is your choice to believe what God says about who you are.

Even knowing all that Christ has done for us, we still deal with the worldly consequences and memories of our sins. Just because you have sinned sexually doesn't mean that a Christian man or woman will never love you. It does mean that you will have to be honest about those mistakes with your future spouse. You have to process this in your mind and heart now in order to be ready for the pitfalls that could possibly await you in the future so that you and your future spouse can avoid them. You can't change the past, but you can start living for God today, keeping Him first in your life and protecting your heart for your spouse.

Acts of Affection vs. Acts of Desire

The Bible gives us two categories for Christian

---

[93] Romans 8:1
[94] 2 Corinthians 5:17

women in relation to Christian men. They are either sisters in Christ or wives. There isn't any other type of relationship that is described. There is no middle ground. Ladies, if a guy says, "Well, it's kind of like we are already married," you say, "It's kind of like we're not!" You are either married or you aren't. There are two types of physical acts in a dating relationship: one that shows emotional affection and one that shows physical desire.

Acts of affection are how you convey that you like, appreciate, respect (for men) and cherish (for women) those that you are dating - just as a mother is affectionate toward her son by hugging him, or a father is affectionate with his daughter by holding her hand or kissing her goodnight. There is nothing sexual in those acts. The point of the act is to communicate that the son and daughter know that they are loved by their parents. Anything that comes after acts of affection are acts of physical desire.

Acts of desire are reserved specifically for marriage because the very purpose is to build the desire to have sex – it's called foreplay. Again, once

> *Keep the fire in the fireplace.*

you start down the physical road, you do not go backwards. Imagine holding in your hand a firecracker and lighting the short fuse. In your mind you think, "When it burns close enough to the firecracker, I will snuff it out." Exciting, right? This is the same condition that exists in even the smallest act of foreplay. It excites, entices and demands the next step; it can be extremely hard to snuff out at before it goes too far. Don't light the fuse, until it is in the right place and time that the explosion will be appropriately enjoyed without causing harm. Some have said, "Keep the fire in the fireplace". In our houses we don't light fires in uncontrolled spaces. In the fireplace, the fire is beautiful and useful. Sexual activity in an uncontrolled space will cause damage. In the fireplace of life-time commitment to each other, and full acknowledgement of responsibility to children born from the moments of passion, the fire is wonderful and useful. The physical relationship always progresses toward sexual release. Remember, the Greek word "porneia" has a broader sense to include everything and anything that might be considered sexually illicit.[95] So while sex outside of marriage is out of bounds, so is everything leading up to sex that could be considered foreplay. Paul reminds us:

> *Flee immorality. Every other sin that a man commits is outside the body, but the immoral man sins against his own body.* [96]

My grandfather had a great saying, "If you have to think about it twice, chances are it is wrong." There is no line drawn in the sand with that statement, just a solid principle. Run from everything that could be

Run from everything that could be considered immoral.

---

[95] Matthew 15:19
[96] 1 Corinthians 6:18

considered immoral or enticing. For some of you, holding hands or a hug is as far as you should go. For others, maybe a kiss goodnight is fine, but as the bride in Song of Solomon says – don't arouse even the desire for the physical before marriage. Build on your friendship and understanding of one another with full confidence that, if you do get married, the physical aspect will come naturally. The bottom line is anything that causes your body to start preparing for sexual activity is too far.

Other Thoughts

This is a tough topic because men and women view this differently. Typically, men are the ones pushing for sex, and women are the ones having to say "no." The main reason for that is, men and women fantasize about different things. Girls, this may disgust you, but guys pretty much only fantasize about sexual foreplay and intercourse. Men think about sex about as often as they breathe. My wife puts it this way to the girls she mentors: guys think about sex as often as women compare themselves to other women. Women, on the other hand, for the most part, fantasize about the wedding and kids. They put their first name with a guy's last name right after meeting him to see how it sounds.

The application is this - develop a plan and stick to it. Both men and women can be aroused by sexual touching and the desire for more, so be open and honest with each other, when you first define the dating relationship and discuss ways that you can plan to avoid sexual temptation at the earliest stages. Peter addresses the feeling of lust when he writes, "As obedient children, do not be conformed to the former lusts which were yours in your ignorance."[97] That is, before we had a relationship with Jesus Christ, we were enslaved to lust. He again speaks on its effects when he says, "Beloved, I urge you as aliens and strangers to abstain from fleshly lusts which wage war against the soul."[98]

That grip of lust can be experienced with many

---

[97] 1 Peter 1:14
[98] 1 Peter 2:11

things – but none is more potent than lust for the opposite sex! Scripture refers to our bodies as flesh (the word used in the Greek is "sarx," which literally means the "meat" in which our souls reside). Our flesh has certain biochemical responses that happen on a daily basis, whether we like it or not. When we see a certain food that we like, there is a biochemical response triggered and we hunger for that food. Likewise, when we see someone to whom we are attracted emotionally and physically, there is a biochemical response that suggests we should satisfy that hunger. That reaction isn't lust, but acting on it is. Much like a car that has a tendency to pull to the right, it is the driver's responsibility to correct the vehicle before it veers off course. In the same way, our bodies were made to respond in a certain way to the opposite sex by our Creator, and we have to deal with those responses appropriately. James tells us that, "Then when lust has conceived, it gives birth to sin; and when sin is accomplished, it brings forth death."[99] So the biochemical response itself is not sin, it is just our

---

[99] James 1:15

body's reaction. The sin comes when we respond inappropriately to our body's reaction. It is also that lust, Peter says, that wages war against us.

By the way, these physiological and emotional responses that were created by God were declared by Him to be very good.[100] God created it to be powerful. It is the dynamo that keeps the population of the earth growing; but it is not so powerful that we cannot master it. It is possible. We are commanded to exercise self-control, which is one of fruits of the Spirit.[101] Look at the passage in Genesis, when God tells Cain, "sin is crouching at the door; and its desire is for you, but you must master it."[102] The same principle applies toward lust and sexuality. We must acknowledge the power of the God-created sex drive in us; but we also need to be self-controlled, with the aid of the Holy Spirit.

If you are to guard your heart, as we learned previously, you must also guard against lust. So, have an agreed upon plan that the two of you decide on, and

---

[100] Genesis 1:31
[101] Galatians 5:22-23
[102] Genesis 4:7

stick to it. If you have spiritual mentors or accountability partners, it would be wise to share what your agreed upon limits are. Request that they ask you on a regular basis how you are keeping to the original plan. We need each other, as trusted agents and protectors of our hearts to win in this area.

Take Home Points:

- *Don't arouse love before its time. Sex was meant for marriage*

- *Even if you have given yourself physically to someone before marriage, God can still use you.*

- *The physical relationship always progresses. There is a line that starts at holding hands and ends at sex. Once you start down that line, you never go back.*

- *If you can't do it in a restaurant, you shouldn't do it in private.*

- *Agree upon a plan to guard against premarital sex during your "D.T.R." and stick to it.*

- *Share your plan with someone who will hold you accountable.*

Chapter 7: Common Questions

*Where there is no guidance the people fall, but
in abundance of counselors there is victory.*
Proverbs 11:14

❦

Now that we have worked through the concepts of viewing dating as an interview for marriage, guarding our hearts and fortifying its protection, you might still be left with some questions. Over the years, we have gotten literally thousands of questions about dating from our college students. Most of them can be distilled into the questions found here. Some of these answers will refer to specific sections in the book, others will supplement the preceding chapters.

How do I know when I'm ready to date?

You are ready to date when you are ready not to – when you have come to the place where you don't just go out with someone for the sake of not being alone, but that you are truly seeking the person you want to marry. When you are ready to say "no" to someone who doesn't meet the requirements your Lord has set before you, then you know you are ready to enter into a dating relationship.

What if I have given myself physically to someone before marriage?

Hewlett-Packard did an internal study that revealed "that women only apply for open jobs if they think they meet 100 percent of the criteria listed. Men apply if they think they meet 60 percent of the requirements." [103] That study explained why the majority of people who ask this question are women.

---

[103] Sandberg, Sheryl. Lean In: Women, Work and the Will to Lead. 2013, p. 145.

Women never think they are good enough and men always shoot above the mark – especially in dating! The enemy will tell you is that you have failed, you're dirty, you're damaged goods and no Christian will want you as a spouse. That is a lie. When you accepted the sacrifice of Jesus on the Cross, His blood paid for your sin. All the dirt and mud of your sin – past, present and future – was washed clean of you. You aren't broken, you've been made new. You aren't damaged goods, you are a new creation.

There is nothing that can protect your mind or your heart from memories of premarital sex. Having sex before marriage will always have consequences at some point in your life, especially in marriage. You can never erase the memories of "going too far" with someone else. God says, "If we confess our sins, He is faithful and righteous to forgive us our sins and to cleanse us from all unrighteousness."[104] If you have put your faith in Jesus, God has forgiven you. To move on in life, you need to acknowledge that what you did was a sin and repent of that sin. You then have to

---

[104] 1 John 1:9

accept God's forgiveness in your life, which also means accepting freedom from guilt and forgiving yourself. Paul held the coats of those that stoned Stephen to death, all the while approving of their actions.[105] He admits to Timothy his regrets of that day,[106] but he doesn't wallow in self-pity over his past sins. Rather, he forces himself to let go of the past and press forward.[107] The blood of Jesus doesn't just cover our sins, it covers our guilt. [108] There is no condemnation in Christ Jesus,[109] and we are a new creation.[110] It is your choice to believe what God says about who you are.

Even knowing all that Christ has done for us, we still deal with the worldly consequences and memories of our sins. Just because you have sinned, doesn't mean that a Christian man or woman will never love you. It does mean that you will have to be honest about those mistakes with your future spouse.

---

[105] Acts 22:19-20
[106] 1 Timothy1:12-15
[107] Philippians 3:13-14
[108] Hebrews 9:14
[109] Romans 8:1
[110] 2 Corinthians 5:17

You can't change the past, but you can start living for God today, keeping Him first in your life and protecting your heart for your spouse.

Can I have a "friend" of the opposite sex?

There are two types of people that ask me about this. The first is someone who isn't dating anyone but has a relationship with a "special friend" of the opposite sex. Let's first define what we are talking about here. I'm not talking about acquaintances, or people you see in class, or work with on projects. Of course that's alright; how could we get anything done otherwise? We are talking about someone that you hang out with on a consistent basis, call and talk to about life's problems, and with whom you regularly share meals together. With all of these activities in play, we need to ensure we are not deceiving ourselves or the other person about the significance of the relationship. Don't confuse being friendly with being a friend. Let's put it this way. If you aren't dating anyone, and you are consistently

> *A dating relationship with a woman takes work. No guy wants to put work into something they don't want to be invested in.*

hanging out with your "friend" and your future spouse walks by, will he or she assume that you are taken? Do other people see you as being a couple? If so, perhaps you should take a step back and rethink your relationship. One or the other of you is probably trying to fill some need in their life without the entanglements of a dating relationship… and it is usually the guy.

The other person that comes to us with this question is someone who is already in a dating relationship with someone who has that "special friend." Girls, unfortunately, are all too often clueless when it comes to these matters. Men always have an ulterior motive, and it is not always sex. Many times guys just want to get the perks of a dating relationship, without the entanglements. They want the girl's affection and to have a good time, without being committed to a set of rules that comes with a dating relationship. Most of the time, guys who want to be friends with a girl who is already in a dating relationship are just waiting for their chance to date her. Recall the chapter on *How Love Works*. It is easier for a guy to have a friendship with another guy. A dating relationship with a woman takes work. No guy wants to put work into something they don't want to be invested in. Also, out of respect, if it bothers the person you are dating, you should re-evaluate both relationships. If the person is worth continuing a dating relationship with, then consider breaking ties with that "special friend." Definitely don't seclude yourself, but be wise with your relationships.

Remember that dating is an interview for marriage. You are interviewing the person to whom you want entrust your heart for the rest of your life. You don't want to entrust it with someone who will be careless with it. When you get married, having friends of the opposite sex is a danger that is too great to chance. Almost every instance of adultery happens with someone who started out as "just a friend."

Can I date my freshman year in college?

Of course you can date as a freshman... if you are ready to get married in the near future, and if you are cautious to be involved with a group of Christian friends. This isn't a rule, but a principle. Remember that your freshman year of college is where you meet new people, become comfortable with who you are, and learn to live life responsibly without your parents. When you enter into a dating relationship, especially for the wrong reasons, there is a tendency to sequester yourself from your friends and other people and just hang out with that person. Also, as a freshman we may establish a dating relationship to replace the affections and friendship we had at home. There may be very little concern for the other person, as long as we are having our "family ties" needs being met, and should the relationship end, it can leave you stranded emotionally.

Should I date more than one person at a time?

The quick, shoot from the hip response for that is, if you have to ask, it is probably wrong. Only out of respect for the person you are dating, you should date only one person at a time. Always stick with "plan A" and never have a "plan B." Don't keep someone in the back of your mind who you would date if the person you are dating now doesn't work out. There is no plan "B." If there is, you need to reevaluate plan "A." Certainly, that is a good practice to be in when you get married.

Is there a right way to break up?

I don't think there is a definite right way to break up, but there are a ton of definite wrong ways to break up. Respect is always the key for guys and girls. If you have correctly defined the relationship, as discussed in the chapter on the Dating Relationship, you would have discussed breaking up and the reasons for doing so. We need to try to be respectful without being hurtful. Go to the other person and say this:

> *I told you from the beginning that I would protect our hearts first and foremost. I said if at any point in time I feel that we aren't right for each other, I would tell you, and we would part ways so that we wouldn't fall into undue temptation. I don't see us getting married, and I don't want to drag this out further and cause either of us to stumble.*

Now, while being far from easy, that is still better that the old "let's just be friends" speech or the "it's not you it's me" line. Remember, part of guarding your heart and the heart of the person you are dating is not hurting them. You want to break up in a way that the person knows it is over, without injuring him or her emotionally.

How far should I take the physical relationship?

Remember that a physical relationship always progresses. You can think about it like a road that starts at holding hands and ends at sexual intercourse. Once you start down that road, you rarely want to go backwards – the physical sexual activity always excites and encourages further activity. You must be sure that you take precautions in your dating relationship to guard against going too far sexually. If you ever say to yourself, or to your date, "just" or "only", as in, "Its *just* one night, and we can handle it," or, "its *only* one step, we won't go farther," you are kidding yourself at best, more likely lying to yourself. Any use of justifying words, like "just" and "only," are yellow warning lights, indicating you know you shouldn't be asking. Paul says, "But put on the Lord Jesus Christ, and make no provision for the flesh in regard to its lusts."[111] This doesn't mean that you draw a legalistic line, walk right up to it consistently and

---

[111] Romans 13:14

hang out there. It means if you both know you have struggled in the past, don't be alone in tempting situations. If you can't do it in a restaurant with everyone watching, it is probably not a good idea to do it at all.

Is kissing okay?

This is usually the follow up to the previous question. Remember the differences between acts of affection and acts of desire. Acts of affection are how you convey that you like or love someone. Acts of desire build the desire to have sex and are reserved specifically for marriage. There is kissing and there is *kissing*. There is a large spectrum between a simple good night kiss, and an exchange of tongues! Some kinds of kissing are clearly more erotic, and encourage further stimulation. Remember, anything that causes your body to start preparing for sex is too far. For some of you, and you know who you are, holding hands or a hug is as far as you should go. For others maybe a kiss goodnight is fine, but as the bride says in Song of

Solomon – don't even arouse the desire for the physical before marriage.[112]

How soon is too soon to get married?

He who finds a wife finds a good thing,
and obtains favor from the LORD.
Proverbs 18:22

You need to temper the reflex to get married as soon as you find the right person with the wisdom of not jumping in too quickly. There are some phenomenal people that have gotten married after knowing each other for only a few weeks and have been married fifty years. As I wrote earlier, dear friends of ours met each other in high school, and at the ages of 18 and 19, right after she graduated, got married and went on a honeymoon to Six Flags. They are still happily married after more than 35 years. I definitely wouldn't recommend that short route for

---

[112] Song of Solomon 8:4

everybody, but it worked for them, because they were walking in obedience to Jesus teachings, and their parents, who knew them better than anyone else, supported the decision. There are people that have dated for years "just to be sure" before getting married whose marriages have failed miserably. In all things you need to ask God with an open and sincere heart when the right timing is; He won't let you down. In general, if you have dated the person for a full year and you both feel God leading you toward marriage, you at least need to have the discussion.

Remember Paul's first letter to the Corinthians. The major Roman port city of Corinth was notorious for debauchery, even in the heathen world. Paul says to the Corinthians:

> *But I say to the unmarried and to widows that it is good for them if they remain even as I. But if they do not have self-control, let them marry; for it is better to marry than to burn with*

passion.[113]

That's far from a negative statement. If you don't have the desire to date or to get married, chances are you aren't reading this book. For the ninety nine percent of us that desire marriage, it is better to marry than to put yourself through prolonged temptation. Here is what I mean by that – my wife and I recently conducted marriage counseling for a couple who had been engaged for over *two years*. They are now happily married, but even they would admit that a long engagement wasn't in their best interest. If you've found a good thing, and if you both know that God wants you together, there needs to be a good reason to continue dating or have a long, drawn out engagement before putting yourself through the temptation. Parents always want their kids to finish college or *fill-in-the-blank*, when in reality they are forcing their children into a prolonged period of temptation. Furthermore, I can't tell you how often I hear about how long it will take to plan a wedding… as if the wedding is more

---

[113] 1 Corinthians 7:8-9

important than the marriage! Weddings are always planned in the first three months and the couple sits around for the rest of the six to twenty four months in temptation. Guard your heart and your spouse's heart, whatever that means for you.

How can I pray for my future spouse?

Praying for your spouse is key. You can pray that God would show you who your spouse is in His timing and that He would protect your heart and your spouse's heart in the process. Pray for your future as a couple – that you would both make positive impact for His kingdom and that your home would honor Him. Pray for faithfulness in your marriage. For guys, pray that God would grow you into the man He needs you to be and the spiritual leader your wife will need (girls, you can pray this for your future husband). For girls, pray that God would grow you into the woman He needs you to be and the Godly woman your husband will need (guys, you can pray this for your future wife). Pray that, if you have children, you would lead them in a Godly way, with wisdom and discernment. Pray that you wouldn't give your heart to anyone but your spouse.

Can a girl to ask a guy out?

Once again, the answer of course is, yes. There is nothing biblically wrong with it, nor is it heretical to do so. A woman *can* ask a guy out on a date. The real question is, *should* a girl ask a guy out on a date. Girls should look for a guy who is a solid Christian who can lead them. In the Bible, there are different roles assigned to men and women. Leadership is the role that is assigned to men; this is true in the church and in the family.[114] It is a wise practice to set yourself up with habits that will enable your marriage, not hinder it. In the dating relationship, men should initiate and women should respond. If he knows you are interested in him, he can't lead in something as simple as asking you out on a date, you shouldn't expect him to lead spiritually in the rest of the relationship. Secondly, you

---

[114] 1 Corinthians 11 and Ephesians 5

might be asking for trouble. If he doesn't like you enough, why would you want to go out on a date with him in the first place?

What does it mean to lead a girl on?

This is a hard one, because it means different things to different women. The question might be better addressed as to how *not* to lead a girl on. The best way is to make your intentions clear. If you find yourself hanging around a girl a lot, or she is hanging around you, be sure to let her know if you are interested in her romantically within the first few weeks. Awkward or not, you never want to keep a girl guessing. The best way to show a girl you are interested is to ask her out on a date, and make sure you use the word "date." Keep your intentions on the front burner and let her know what is going on with you regularly. If you aren't interested in her, or if you know she isn't the one, let her know quickly and respectfully.

What is a "Spiritual Leader" in a dating relationship?

There is an old saying, "Leave it better than you found it." As Christians, we need to better those around us. The Bible says, "Iron sharpens iron, so one man sharpens another."[115] We can't do anything that would lead our brothers or sisters in Christ astray from the Lord. When and if the two of you part ways, you need to leave that person closer to Jesus than when you started dating. This doesn't mean you have to pray with them and have a Bible study on a daily basis (in fact, I would be very cautious about doing so, because prayer and study in God's word can lead to a personal intimacy you probably aren't ready for before marriage). What it does mean is that you don't constantly push them in the physical realm, either tempting them visually or physically. It means that you should encourage their walk with the Lord, encourage them to have Godly friends and to find a good church home. You should enable them to spend time with the

---

[115] Proverbs 27:17

Lord, not keep them from that time. Be the communicator and the initiator. In everything, you need to be confident that if you ever meet his or her spouse you could confidently look them in the eye.

(Guys) How can I pursue a girl?

First and foremost, ask her out on a date, call it a date, and pay for the date. Then let her know your intentions and how you feel about her. Don't keep her guessing; keep your intentions clear. Be honest about how you feel and have those mini "DTRs" to keep you both on the same page. Listen to what she says. Take interest in what she is interested in.

(Girls) How can I pursue a guy?

With *reservation*. Let me say that again, be reserved. Never throw yourself at a man. Men are hunters. They like to pursue. So what does that look like? Ruth made herself available without appearing needy. She put herself where Boaz was. She placed herself in his sphere of influence. Hang around. Be available to go places with him. If he works at a restaurant, sit at his table. If He works at the library, read a book in his section. Try to be in his sphere of influence without being a stalker.

What about "Mission Dates?"

This has "bad idea" written all over it - from both sides. For those of you who are clueless as to what I'm talking about, I'll explain. A mission date is where you go on a date with someone who isn't a Christian under the supposed auspices of sharing Christ with them. In reality, it is usually an excuse to go out with someone you know you shouldn't be going out with in the first place. Look at it this way: you are in a company and want to locate and interview an electrical engineer to join the company. There is an applicant who is an English teacher who has applied for the job. You know, regardless of how smart and capable this worker may be, they are not going to be an effective electrical engineer. Why would you waste your time and theirs doing an interview? Similarly, why would we entertain the non-Christian interviewee as a potential spouse when we know they do not fit the job qualifications in the most essential categories? We would not conduct spurious interviews in any other endeavor, why would we then in such an important area of our life?

If the purpose of dating is an interview to find your spouse, and the Bible is clear on not marrying a non-believer, why put yourself through more temptation? We need to guard our hearts and the hearts of those around us, especially those we date. Leading someone on in order to "share the Gospel" with them isn't exactly living out Christ. In fact, it is really lying to them by telling them you are interested in them when, in reality, you aren't. Finally, if your future spouse sees you with that person, what will he or she think?

How do I know if he or she is the one?

This is perhaps the most difficult question to

answer, and ultimately, through much prayer and counsel, it can only be answered by you. From the moment I met my wife Amanda, I wanted to be around her. Even after dating her for a year, I never got tired of her presence. When we would go on trips separately with our families, both of us would long to be with each other. I can remember one time specifically on spring break when I was at home and Amanda was on vacation with her family. She called me every day, and while we both enjoyed spending time with our families, we longed for the other person to be there with us. So the first thing I usually ask when I get this question is, "Do you hate being apart, or is distance welcome?" Remember, you will be spending a long time with the person you marry, so you want to enjoy your time together.

Consider seeking wise counsel from Christians that know you well. Over the years, my wife and I have listened to many unhappy couples who jumped into marriage too quickly, didn't listen to or seek sound advice from friends and family, later confessing that they didn't see or deliberately ignore what others tried to warn them about. The way of a fool is right in his own eyes, but a wise man is he who listens to counsel.[116] Where there is no guidance the people fall, but in abundance of counselors there is victory.[117] Find someone that you trust and ask them if the person you are dating seems right for you. Give them a chance to meet the person and see the two of you interact. If your parents have been good counselors for you in the past, and you have generally respected their opinions and counsel, this would be a great time to seek their counsel again. No one knows you more thoroughly than your parents. Introduce him or her to them, and let them get to know the person to see if they complement you.

---

[116] Proverbs 12:15
[117] Proverbs 11:14